BEST OF

Prague

Richard Watkins

How to use this book

Colour-Coding & Maps

Each chapter has a colour code along the banner at the top of the page which is also used for text and symbols on maps (eg all venues reviewed in the Highlights chapter are orange on the maps). The fold-out maps inside the front and back covers are numbered from 1 to 8. All sights and venues in the text have map references; eg (5, B2) means Map 5, grid reference B2. See p128 for map symbols.

Prices

Multiple prices listed with reviews (eg €10/5) usually indicate adult/concession admission to a venue. Concession prices can include senior, student, member or coupon discounts. Meal cost and room rate categories are listed at the start of the Eating and Sleeping chapters, respectively.

Text Symbols

- ☎ telephone
- ✉ address
- ▣ email/website address
- $ admission
- ◷ opening hours
- ⓘ information
- Ⓜ metro
- Ⓣ tram
- Ⓟ parking available
- ♿ wheelchair access
- ✖ on-site/nearby eatery
- ♨ child-friendly venue
- Ⓥ good vegetarian selection

Best of Prague
3rd edition – March 2006
First published – May 2002

Published by Lonely Planet Publications Pty Ltd
ABN 36 005 607 983

Australia	Head Office, Locked Bag 1, Footscray, Vic 3011
	☎ 03 8379 8000, fax 03 8379 8111
	▣ talk2us@lonelyplanet.com.au
USA	150 Linden St, Oakland, CA 94607
	☎ 510 893 8555, toll free 800 275 8555
	fax 510 893 8572
	▣ info@lonelyplanet.com
UK	72–82 Rosebery Ave, Clerkenwell, London EC1R 4RW
	☎ 020 7841 9000, fax 020 7841 9001
	▣ go@lonelyplanet.co.uk

This title was commissioned in Lonely Planet's London office and produced by: **Commissioning Editor** Judith Bamber **Coordinating Editors** Victoria Harrison, Margedd Heliosz **Coordinating Cartographer** Anthony Phelan **Layout Designer** Indra Kilfoyle **Cartographers** Valentina Kremencutskaya, Jacqui Saunders & Emma McNicol **Managing Cartographer** Mark Griffiths **Cover Designer** Annika Roojun **Project Managers** Fabrice Rocher, Eoin Dunlevy **Mapping Development** Paul Piaia **Desktop Publishing Support** Mark Germanchis **Thanks to** Glenn Beanland, Carol Chandler, Sally Darmody, Brendan Dempsey, Michala Green, Imogen Hall, Adriana Mammarella, Stephanie Pearson, Gerard Walker, Celia Wood

© Lonely Planet Publications Pty Ltd 2006.

Photographs by Lonely Planet Images and Richard Nebesky except for the following: p10 Brent Winebrenner, p22 Cheryl Conlon, p26 & p35 Izzet Keribar, p39 Oliver Strewe, p49 Martin Moos, p51 Witold Skrypczak, p66 Chris Mellor, p81 Doug McKinlay, p100 Jonathan Smith **Cover photograph** The beautifully styled Astronomical Clock dating from the 1400s, Stephen Simpson/Getty Images. All images are copyright of the photographers unless otherwise indicated. Many of the images in this guide are available for licensing from Lonely Planet Images: www.lonelyplanetimages.com.

ISBN 1 74059 711 7

Printed through Colorcraft Ltd, Hong Kong.

Printed in China

Acknowledgments Prague Metro Map © DP Praha, akciová společnost

Contents

From the Publisher

THE AUTHOR
Richard Watkins

Richard was born and bred in Wales and after five years studying decided he'd like to see more of the world, which he's now been doing for several years. On his first trip to Prague, Richard was immediately captivated by the Czech capital's preponderance for off-the-wall surrealism, cool jazz, grand opera and cheap beer.

Thanks are due to staff at the Czech Embassy in London and the Czech Tourist Authority. Also to Jaroslava Nováková at the Prague Information Centre, Jaromír Kubúo at Karlštejn Castle, and Jane Rawson

The 1st edition of this book was written by Paul Smitz. The 2nd edition was written by Richard Watkins.

LONELY PLANET AUTHORS

Why is our travel information the best in the world? It's simple: our authors are independent, dedicated travellers. They don't research using just the Internet or phone, and they don't take freebies in exchange for positive coverage. They travel widely, to all the popular spots and off the beaten track. They personally visit thousands of hotels, restaurants, cafés, bars, galleries, palaces, museums and more – and they take pride in getting all the details right, and telling it how it is. For more, see the authors section on **www.lonelyplanet.com**.

PHOTOGRAPHER
Richard Nebesky

Richard was not born with a camera in his hand; however, it wasn't long before his father, an avid photo enthusiast, gave him his first happy-snap unit. Ever since then the camera has been by his side. Richard has researched, written and photographed for numerous Lonely Planet guides as well as for various magazines and other travel guidebook publishers.

SEND US YOUR FEEDBACK

We love to hear from travellers – your comments keep us on our toes and help make our books better. Our well-travelled team reads every word on what you loved or loathed about this book. Although we cannot reply individually to postal submissions, we always guarantee that your feedback goes straight to the appropriate authors, in time for the next edition – and the most useful submissions are rewarded with a free book. To send us your updates – and find out about Lonely Planet events, newsletters and travel news – visit our award-winning website: **www.lonelyplanet.com/feedback**.

Note: we may edit, reproduce and incorporate your comments in Lonely Planet products such as guidebooks, websites and digital products, so let us know if you don't want your comments reproduced or your name acknowledged. For a copy of our privacy policy visit **www.lonelyplanet.com/privacy**.

Introducing Prague

At the heart of Europe, Prague is one of the continent's most historically rich cities. Over the last thousand years it has been the seat of Bohemian kings, the capital of the Holy Roman Empire and one of the jewels of the Habsburg Empire, and its grandeur remains undiminished today.

Modern Prague is a colourful and dynamic place. Its boulevards and laneways have outstanding combinations of the classically old and the startlingly modern. Grandly preserved baroque buildings host stylish bars and restaurants, while stucco-encrusted theatres and Romanesque cellars echo with the sounds of orchestras, string quartets and the coolest jazz around.

Prague's magnificent castle is clearly its main draw, but there are numerous art galleries, museums, churches and synagogues jostling for your attention, countless pubs in which to seek refreshment afterwards, and music everywhere, from the Charles Bridge buskers to the classical concerts, jazz clubs and international pop acts around town. In fact, there's so much going on you'll be positively spoilt for choice.

The city viewed from the terrace of a restaurant in Mala Strana

Neighbourhoods

Prague sits astride the Czech Republic's longest river, the Vltava, and is divided into 10 districts, each comprising a number of suburbs. The compact historical centre (Praha 1) is the hub of most tourist activity and is itself made up of five distinct neighbourhoods. At the heart of Prague is **Staré Město** (Old Town), stretching from the Vltava east to náměstí Republiky, north to Široká and Dlouhá, and south to Národní. The beautiful Staroměstské náměstí (Old Town Square) is home to the Astronomical Clock and the Týn Church, with its cobblestone lanes threading their way to Charles Bridge. To the north is **Josefov**, centre of Prague's Jewish community. The main attraction is the Jewish Museum and the Old-New Synagogue. South and east of the Old Town lies **Nové Město** (New Town), a commercial area with more recent historical attractions such as the National Museum, plus lively clubs, bars and restaurants west of the city's main shopping drag, Wenceslas Square.

Vinohrady, southeast of the main train station, is filled with lots of fashionable eateries and bars, and some of Prague's glitziest shopping malls. To the northeast is **Žižkov**, a grungy area with cheap accommodation and alternative-scene bars and clubs. South of New Town is Prague's ethereal second castle, **Vyšehrad**, and across the river is the up-and-coming suburb of **Smíchov**. This old industrial quarter is having a major facelift, complete with giant shopping malls. A warren of picturesque streets, stunning vistas and a lively restaurant scene can be found at **Malá Strana** (Small Quarter).

A spectacular castle dominates the heights of **Hradčany**, further to the northwest. In the opposite direction, on the Vltava's 'big bend', is the parkland swathe of **Letná**, which is bordered by **Bubeneč**, a one-time fishing village that features Prague's largest park, Stromovka. Finally, in the northeast, you'll enjoy an eclectic mix of fairgrounds, museums and galleries in **Holešovice**.

OFF THE BEATEN TRACK

Try the peaceful, leafy grounds of **Vyšehrad** (p23) for a quick trip into quietude or, better still, the vast expanse of **Stromovka** (p37) where camera-happy crowds are thankfully unknown. If you're in search of a quiet meal or liquid refreshment away from the tour groups, drop by **Restaurace Podskalská Celnice Na Výtoni** (p74). The **Lapidárium** (p26), **Army Museum** (p26) and **Troja Chateau** (p30) are among the less visited of Prague's attractions, while Vinohrady, with its numerous restaurants, and Smíchov, home to the famous Staropramen Brewery (and Na Verandách restaurant; see p80) and Prague's biggest and glossiest shopping mall, are largely tourist free.

Relax at baroque Troja Chateau

Itineraries

Prague is one of Europe's best preserved medieval cities – its unrivalled wealth of baroque, Art Nouveau and, uniquely, cubist architecture were good enough reasons for Unesco to add the city's historic centre to its World Cultural Heritage list in 1992. Prague is filled with amazing museums and art galleries, and has some truly outstanding sights, such as the magnificent Prague Castle, Týn Church, with its spires poking above the rooftops, and the stately elegance of Charles Bridge. So grab a Prague Card (see p114) and hit the streets on one of the following itineraries.

WORST OF PRAGUE
- blister-inducing cobblestones
- endless traffic on the main roads
- dodging shuffling crowds of camcorder-wielding tourists in the Old Town
- stodgy dumplings
- the overabundance of tacky souvenir shops
- stag and hen parties

One Day

Head straight to Old Town Square, and watch the Astronomical Clock do its thing. Cross Charles Bridge and climb to the imposing Prague Castle, where St Vitus Cathedral and the Royal Garden await. Make your way back to Malostranské náměstí in the evening for a meal at Square.

Two Days

Explore the synagogues and the Old Jewish Cemetery of Josefov, and drop by Bakeshop Praha for coffee and cake. Take a leisurely walk along the river, and maybe go to a concert at the Rudolfinum, followed by dinner at Don Pedro or La Perle de Prague.

Three Days

Head north of the river and immerse yourself in cutting-edge culture at the huge Centre for Modern & Contemporary Art. Afterwards, wander through Stromovka park, or Letná Gardens, and take in the wonderful city views in the company of a couple of well-earned beers.

Seek out the Singing Fountain (p37) in Prague's Royal Garden

Highlights

PRAGUE CASTLE & ST VITUS CATHEDRAL (8)

Commanding the skyline above the Vltava, **Prague Castle** (Pražský Hrad) is undoubtedly the brightest jewel the Czech capital has to offer. This vast walled compound has a tumultuous 1100-year history and a scale that qualifies it as the biggest ancient castle in the world. There is so much to see, you could easily spend a whole day here, though its status as Prague's premier tourist draw means you'll be sharing it with the teeming hordes at pretty much any time. The Czech Republic's largest church, **St Vitus Cathedral**, rises up inside the castle walls.

Prince Bořivoj erected the first fortified settlement on this site back in the 9th century, and the stronghold expanded over the ensuing centuries, hence the mixture of architectural styles from Romanesque to Art Nouveau. Renovations began in the 12th century with the Romanesque features added by Prince Sobešlav I, and one of the oldest extant parts of the castle is the **Old Royal Palace** (p27), dating from 1135 and famous for its wonderful late Gothic vaulted roof. The **Basilica of St George** (p32) dates back even further, to the 10th century, though it was heavily restored in the 19th century.

Other star sights include the fascinating exhibition on the castle's history, **The Story of Prague Castle** (p28), the museum of Czech history in the **Lobkowicz Palace** (p26), the collection of Bohemian art in the **Convent of St George** (p28) and the assembly of Old Masters at the **Prague Castle Gallery** (p29). Also worth a look are the **Toy Museum** (p43), the **Powder Tower** (p32) and **Golden Lane** (p39), while the **Royal Garden** (p36), with its Renaissance **Summer Palace** (p30) and the formal **Garden on the Ramparts** (p36),

INFORMATION

- ☎ 224 373 368
- 🖥 www.prague.cz/prague-castle
- ✉ Hradčany
- € Ticket A (St Vitus Cathedral, Old Royal Palace, Basilica of St George, Convent of St George, The Story of Prague Castle, Powder Tower & Golden Lane) 350/175Kč; 220/110Kč Ticket B (St Vitus Cathedral, Old Royal Palace & Golden Lane); 50Kč Ticket C (Golden Lane); 50/25Kč Ticket D (Basilica of St George); 50/25Kč Ticket E (Powder Tower); 100/50Kč Ticket F (Convent of St George); grounds admission free
- 🕙 historic buildings 9am-5pm Apr-Oct, 9am-4pm Nov-Mar; grounds 5am-midnight Apr-Oct, 6am-11pm Nov-Mar
- ℹ️ information centre open 9am-5pm Apr-Oct, 9am-4pm Nov-Mar; audio guide per 2/3hr 145/180Kč; guided tours (90Kč) 9am-4pm Tue-Sun
- Ⓜ Malostranská or Hradčanská
- ♿ limited
- 🍴 U Labutí (p67)

Dizzying heights of Gothic spires

They're changing guards at Prague Castle

offers a leafy respite from the crowds. The changing of the guard happens on the hour, at the main gate on **Hradčanské náměstí** (p37).

St Vitus Cathedral (Katedrála Sv Vita) rears above the third courtyard of Prague Castle, with its lofty 100m main tower and amazing 10.5m-diameter rose window. Emperor Charles IV initiated construction in 1344 on the site of a 10th-century rotunda, but it wasn't until thousands of pieces of glass had been painstakingly set in the large west-facing rose window in 1929 that St Vitus was finally completed.

The cathedral's huge nave is encircled by side-chapels, the most striking of which is the **Chapel of St Wenceslas** with its walls of polished semiprecious stones. Even more ostentatious is the ultra-baroque silver tomb of **St John of Nepomuk**, surrounded by silver angels. Beneath the floor of the cathedral is the **Royal Crypt**, a tight space (particularly when jammed with fellow visitors) with little to see other than the 1930s sarcophagi holding the remains of Charles IV, Wenceslas IV, Rudolf II and George of Poděbrady. If you have a head for heights, you might care to scale the tower for the great views at the top, but be prepared for 287 slow, strenuous steps.

STAINED IN STYLE

St Vitus Cathedral is blessed with some exemplary stained-glass windows. Most spectacular is that by Art Nouveau artist Alfons Mucha (1909) in the New Archbishop's Chapel. For some of the oldest examples, see the three windows in the Chapel of St Antony (1865–66); for one of the newest, see the window in the southern wall of the Chapel of St Wenceslas (1968).

OLD TOWN SQUARE & ASTRONOMICAL CLOCK (7, C2)

At the heart of the Old Town, **Old Town Square** (Staroměstské Náměstí), surrounded by elegant baroque, rococo and Gothic architecture, is a visually stunning space, focused on the dramatic **Jan Hus Statue** (p31). It has been Prague's principal public centre since the 10th century. These days it's the hub of the tourist industry, filled with overpriced cafés, tacky souvenir stalls and horse-drawn carriages waiting for business. However, no amount of commercialism can detract from one of Europe's loveliest urban spaces.

To the east rise the spires of the Gothic **Church of Our Lady Before Týn** (p22); nearby are the rococo **Kinský Palace** (p29) and the medieval **House at the Stone Bell** (p29). At the northwestern edge is the baroque **St Nicholas Church** (p25).

The **Old Town Hall** (p27), built in 1338, is a complex of homes that were incorporated and rebuilt over many years. The building covered with *sgraffito* (multilayered murals) at the Malé náměstí end was once home to a young Franz Kafka. Perched on the tower is the beautiful **Astronomical Clock**, created in 1490 by a certain Master Hanuš, and graced with representations of astronomical movement and allegorical figures. These are joined on the hour by a parade of apostles for a brief mechanical show. Huge crowds gather well in advance to watch this performance, though it's something of an anticlimax watching the wooden dummies quickly glide past the two opened windows. Nevertheless, it rarely fails to elicit 'oohs', 'aahs' and camera flashes from the expectant spectators.

> ### DON'T MISS
> • exhibitions at the House at the Golden Ring (p28) or Kinský Palace (p29)
> • watching the wooden apostles on the Astronomical Clock nod past on the hour
> • the view from the Old Town Hall tower (p27)

> ### INFORMATION
> ✉ Staroměstské náměstí, Staré Město
> Ⓜ Staroměstská; Můstek
> ♿ good
> ✗ Ambiente Ristorante Pasta Fresca (p74)

The heartbeat of a city – the Old Town Square

CHARLES BRIDGE (4, B3-B4)

This stately, statue-lined bridge spanning the Vltava was commissioned by Charles IV in 1357 to replace the 12th-century Judith Bridge, which had been washed away in a flood some years previously. It was completed in 1402, and for the next 460-odd years **Charles Bridge** (Karlův most) was the only river crossing in Prague. Some 520m in length, the structure was originally simply called the Stone Bridge, and was renamed in honour of Emperor Charles IV in 1870.

The oldest sculpture here is the **Crucifix** (1657), near the Staré Město end. The gilded Hebrew inscription, reading 'Holy, holy, holy, the Lord of Hosts' was funded in 1694 by the fine of a local Jew, Elias Backoffen, who had allegedly mocked it. Most attention goes to the bronze **statue of St John of Nepomuk** (1683), the Czech patron saint who ended up lifeless in the Vltava at the behest of bad King Wenceslas IV in 1393, following a messy court intrigue. Legend says that if you rub the bronze plaque at the base of the statue, you will be sure to return one day to Prague, and countless tourists' palms have given the panel a bright golden sheen.

Other noteworthy monuments include statues of St Wenceslas as a boy (c 1730), St Vitus (1714) and the Vision of St Luitgard (1710). At either end of the bridge is a tower; both are open to visitors and command incredible views from their rooftops, best appreciated in the early dawn light.

> **INFORMATION**
> ✉ Karlův most, Staré Město
> ⓘ Prague Information Service office at the bridge tower on the Malá Strana side of the Vltava
> Ⓜ Staroměstská
> ♿ good
> ✕ Kampa Park (p70)

Soothing the bridge over troubled waters

> **DON'T MISS**
> • the night-time view of a glowing Prague, with silhouetted statues in the foreground
> • listening to a jazz band in the early evening
> • the view from the Staré Město bridge tower

So popular has the bridge become that for much of the day just getting across it can be a struggle, as it fills with crowds shuffling, taking photos and congregating around the souvenir stalls, buskers and caricaturists. However, the views are magnificent, and the jazz bands add an atmospheric swing to the scene.

JEWISH MUSEUM & OLD-NEW SYNAGOGUE (4, D2)

Jews are thought to have settled in Prague as early as the 10th century, though an area known as Jewish Town (later Josefov; p40) was not established until around 200 years later. Founded in 1906, the city's **Jewish Museum** (Židovské Muzeum) today manages seven separate sites in Josefov. These haunting monuments only survived the horrors of WWII because the Nazis planned to create a 'museum of an extinct race' here, and the museum's collections were greatly increased with plunder from the decimated Jewish communities across Bohemia and Moravia.

The **Spanish Synagogue** (p35), with its 'Moorish' design, is one of the more visually striking of Prague's major synagogues, and the museum's main ticket office is located here. Round the back, the **Robert Guttmann Gallery** (p29) stages temporary art exhibitions.

INFORMATION

- ☎ museum 222 317 191
- 🖥 www.jewishmuseum.cz
- ✉ Jewish Museum Reservation Centre, U Starého hřbitova 3a, Josefov; Old-New Synagogue, Červená 1, Josefov
- € museum 300/200Kč; synagogue 200/140Kč
- ☷ museum 9am-6pm Sun-Fri Apr-Oct, 9am-4.30pm Sun-Fri Nov-Mar; synagogue 9.30am-6pm Sun-Thu, 9.30am-5pm Fri Apr-Oct, 9.30am-5pm Sun-Thu, 9.30am-2pm Fri Nov-Mar; both closed on Jewish holidays
- Ⓜ Staroměstská
- ✗ King Solomon (p68)

The **Maisel Synagogue** (p34) has displays on the history of the Jews in Bohemia, while the **Pinkas Synagogue** (p34) to the north is kept as a memorial to the Bohemian and Moravian Jews who died in the Holocaust. The **Klausen Synagogue** (p34) holds an exhibition on Jewish traditions. Nearby are the **Ceremonial Hall** (p26) and the adjoining **Old Jewish Cemetery** (p32).

THE LEGEND OF GOLEM

Of all the many rabbis who have preached at the Old-New Synagogue, Rabbi Loew was the most famous. Legend has it that Loew fashioned Golem – a living creature – from clay to help protect the Jewish community. However, Golem was unstable and after the rabbi forgot to give him his daily orders, he ran amok. Loew was forced to 'undo' Golem, after which he placed the now lifeless clay in the synagogue's attic, though these remains have yet to be found...

The separately run **Old-New Synagogue** (Staronová Synagóga) is the oldest synagogue in Europe, erected in Gothic style around 1270 to serve as Prague's prime site of Jewish worship. Originally called the New (Great) Shul, and subsequently labelled 'Old-New' once other synagogues appeared, the building on Červená is believed to have been predated by an important synagogue called Old Shul, which was demolished in 1867.

The Old-New Synagogue has the twin naves which are typical of secular and sacred medieval architecture, and a half-dozen bays with ribbed vaulting. On the eastern wall is the **holy ark** in which the Torah scrolls are kept. The centre of the synagogue features the **bema** (raised platform supporting a pulpit), enclosed by a 15th-century iron grille, and on the walls are 17th-century Hebrew scriptures.

Star of David at the Old-New Synagogue

Men entering the Old-New Synagogue or the Old Jewish Cemetery must have their heads covered – paper yarmulkes are handed out at the entrances, though hats or bandannas are allowed instead.

Tumbling tombstones in the Old Jewish Cemetery

CENTRE FOR MODERN & CONTEMPORARY ART (6, D3)

The huge, concrete **Trade Fair Palace** (Veletržní palác) in Holešovice was built in 1928 in the new 'functionalist' style. On the outside it's plain and boring, but the stark and spacious white interior provides an ideal setting for Prague's largest and most important collection of modern art.

There are four permanent collections, displayed on levels 1 to 4 (the ground floor, mezzanine level and level 5 host temporary exhibitions). Level 1 is devoted to **20th-century foreign art**, including works by Picasso, Edvard Munch and Gustav Klimt, whose *Virgin* easily steals the show. Level 2 provides an overview of **20th-century Czech art**, from the Daliesque fantasies of František Janoušek to the surreal symbolism of 'Czech Grotesque', a satirical art movement that flourished under the communist regime.

> **DON'T MISS**
> • Picasso's *Self Portrait*
> • Braque's *Still Life with Guitar 1*
> • Emil Filla's *Reader of Dostoyevsky*
> • Van Gogh's *Green Wheat*
> • Rodin's male nude, *The Bronze Age*

> **INFORMATION**
> ☎ 224 301 111
> 🖥 www.ngprague.cz
> ✉ Dukelských hrdinů 47, Holešovice
> € 4 levels 250/120Kč, 3 levels 200/100Kč, 2 levels 150/70Kč, 1 level 100/50Kč, free 1st Wed of month
> 🕑 10am-6pm Tue-Sun (to 9pm Thu)
> ⓘ free audio guide
> Ⓜ Vltavská
> ♿ excellent
> ✂ Corso (p80)

Flamboyant cubist furniture is displayed in the **1900 to 1930 art** section on level 3, while pre-cubist paintings by Emil Filla hang alongside some curious later works such as *Mummy, Mummy, the Cows are Wrestling*. Don't miss Jan Zrzavý's *Cleopatra*, imagined as a kind of shiny red jelly-baby. Also on this floor is the excellent collection of **19th- and 20th-century French art**, with bronzes by Rodin and paintings by Gauguin, Monet, Renoir and others. Toulouse-Lautrec's *At the Moulin Rouge* includes a portrait of Oscar Wilde. More Picassos are shown here too, as well as a scenography exhibition.

Level 4 showcases **19th-century Czech art**, with portraits by Josef Mánes, and humorous 'genre scenes' by his brother, Quido. Bedřich Havránek's finely detailed *By the Brook* and Julius Mařák's woodland scenes typify the rural nostalgia of the period.

MUNICIPAL HOUSE (7, F2)

Prague's most exuberant Art Nouveau palace, the splendid **Municipal House** (Obecní Dům) surprises and delights visitors with its sheer size and elegance. The 500-room landmark was built between 1905 and 1912 on the site of the medieval Royal Court, the official residence of the Bohemian kings from the late 14th century until the Habsburgs moved into the area in 1526. It was intended to impress, as the centre of Czech cultural life in a Prague which was dominated by the German language and cultue. Many leading painters and sculptors were commissioned to create a lavish masterpiece; among the famous names who contributed to the building's magnificence were Alfons Mucha, Karel Špillar, Josef Myslbek and Jan Preisler.

INFORMATION

- ☎ 222 002 101
- 🖥 www.obecnidum.cz
- ✉ náměstí Republiky 5, Staré Město
- € guided tours 150Kč
- 🕙 7.30am-11pm
- ℹ guided tours from information centre (open 10am-6pm); classical music concerts in Smetana Hall
- Ⓜ Náměstí Republiky
- ♿ good
- ✗ Kavárna obecní dům (p76); Francouzská (p76)

While the façade is amazing enough, festooned with sculpted allegorical figures, stucco medallions and a wonderful mosaic lunette, taking centre stage inside is the biggest concert hall in town, **Smetana Hall**. Alive with frescoes, sculptures and natural light from the original skylights, it was here that Czechoslovak independence was declared in 1918. Just off the hall are the restored **Ladies' Withdrawing Room** and Moroccan-style **Oriental Salon**. The **Mayor's Salon** is a veritable gallery of Alfons Mucha's work, dominated by the magestic ceiling fresco *Slavic Concorde,* which depicts an eagle metaphorically held aloft by Czech-personified human virtues. Mucha also designed the stained-glass windows and curtains.

DON'T MISS

- Jan Preisler's murals in the Oriental Salon
- the ceramic tiling lining the stairwell to the basement
- coffee in Kavárna obecní dům
- the Prague Symphony Orchestra in Smetana Hall (p92)

Further along is **Rieger Hall**, where Havel and his associates worked out the handover of power with the communists in 1989.

The Art Nouveau theme is continued in the Hall's three restaurants, most notably in the upmarket **Francouzská**, with a lighter touch in the more casual *kavárna* (café).

NATIONAL MUSEUM (4, G6)

The brooding bulk of the **National Museum** (Národní Muzeum), with its vast natural history collections, rears up at the southern end of Wenceslas Square. Established as the Patriotic Museum in 1818, the museum is the oldest in the Czech Republic, and has occupied this commanding site since 1891.

INFORMATION

- ☎ 224 497 111
- 🖥 www.nm.cz
- ✉ Václavské náměstí 68, Nové Město
- € 100/50Kč, children under 6 free; free 1st Mon of month
- ☉ 10am-6pm May-Sep, 9am-5pm Oct-Apr, closed 1st Tue of month
- ⓘ audio guides 200/150Kč
- Ⓜ Muzeum
- ♿ good
- ✗ on-site café

Brass-handled cabinets and didactic displays create a slightly old-fashioned atmosphere, but the gift shop sells excellent guide-books (99Kč).

The permanent galleries begin on the 1st floor with the **Pantheon**, lined with the bronze likenesses of prominent Czechs such as Jan Hus, Dvořák, Smetana and TG Masaryk. The fusty and seemingly endless **mineralogy** section can cause drowsiness, but it does have some sparkling amethyst crystals. More engaging are the **zoology** and **palaeontology** galleries with their stuffed, glassy-eyed residents, in-cluding an elephant and a giraffe, numerous fossils and gigantic fin whale skeleton, brought here from Norway in 1885.

A tiny **anthropology** gallery has a gruesome collection of human skulls showing diseases, such as syphilis. The National Museum is enlivened with temporary ex-hibitions, which have followed such curiously diverse themes as the history of Czech cinema and the culture of Taiwan, while the atrium is also a venue for regular con-certs. Don't miss the panoramic views of Wenceslas Square from the upper floors.

STUDENT SACRIFICE

It was in front of the National Museum on 16 January 1969 that the 21-year-old Charles University student Jan Palach made the ultimate sacrifice in protest against the Soviet invasion and occupation of his country. Setting himself on fire, he stumbled down the steps in flames and collapsed at the bottom; a cross in the pavement marks the spot where he fell. He died in hospital four days later, and has since been honoured with the renamed Jan Palach Square (p38).

MUSEUM OF CZECH CUBISM (7, E2)

The cubist movement, developed by artists such as Picasso and Braque in the early 20th century, found fertile ground in the Czech lands, where it flourished from around 1910 to 1920. Here it was applied to everything from tea cups and sofas to whole buildings. Prague is the only place in the world where you'll find cubist architecture, the finest example of which, the **House of the Black Madonna** (Dům U Černé Matky Boží), designed by Josef Gočár in 1912, is now home to the fascinating **Museum of Czech Cubism** (Muzeum Českého Kubismu).

> ## INFORMATION
> ☎ 224 211 746
> 🖳 www.ngprague.cz
> ✉ Ovocný trh 19, Staré Město
> € 100/50Kč
> ⏱ 10am-6pm Tue-Sun
> Ⓜ Náměstí Republiky
> ♿ good
> ✗ Grand Café Orient (p76)

The exhibition begins on the 2nd floor with paintings by leading exponents, including Emil Filla and Bohumil Kubišta. Filla's *Writer* (1912) and *Reader* (1913) are among the highlights. Also here are bronze sculptures by Otto Gutfreund, ceramic coffee sets and vases by Pavel Janák and furniture designed by Josef Gočár. The gigantic sofa he created in 1913, for the actor Otto Boleška, is hard to miss.

More painters are represented on the 3rd floor, including the prolific Josef Čapek, Vincenc Beneš and Otakar Kubin, while Vąlav Špála's *Song of Spring* (1915) and Pavel Janák's angular armchairs, desk and bookcase (1912–13) are certainly eye-catching creations.

The 4th floor shows temporary exhibitions and on the 1st floor is the recently reopened **Grand Café Orient** (p76), whose interior fittings were also designed by the very talented Mr Gočár.

CUBIST PRAGUE

Nowhere else will you find genuine cubist architecture, so take the opportunity to track down some of these angular structures. Apart from the House of the Black Madonna, good examples include the **Diamant Building** (4, D6; Spálená 4), **Villa Libušina** (6, C5; cnr Vnislavova & Rašínovo nábřeží), the **Legiobank** (4, G2-H2; Na Poříčí 24) and the unnamed **apartment block** (4, D2; Elišky Krasnohorské 10-14). Also well worth a look is the curious **cubist lamppost** (4, E5; Jungmannovo náměstí). It's one of a kind.

PETŘÍN HILL (5, A5)

After a couple of days traipsing through the crowded Old Town, you'll probably be ready for some green open spaces. **Petřín Hill** (Petřínské sady) is the large mound looming above Malá Strana, and is a peaceful and relaxing place to 'get away from it all', settle down with a good book, or just wander the leafy trails that crisscross its surface.

INFORMATION

- ✉ Petřín Hill, Malá Strana
- ℹ funicular (14/7Kč) runs every 10min 9am-11.30pm, (travel pass for metro, trams and buses can also be used)
- Ⓜ Národní Třída, then tram 22, 23 or 57 to Újezd
- ✖ Cantina (p69)

Why not ride the funicular?

If you've chosen to ride the **funicular** up from Újezd, you can either disembark halfway up the 318m hill and continue on foot, or head to the terminus, emerging at a pretty, formal rose garden. Off to your left you'll find the **Štefánik Observatory** (p43) while the centrepiece of the park is the **Petřín Tower**. This 62m tower is a scale model (5:1) of the Eiffel Tower, built in 1891 for the Prague Exposition, and has spectacular views from the top of its 299 steps. Nearby, kids (and some grown-ups) will love distorting themselves in the **Maze** (p42). In between are 14 giant slabs dating from 1836, and painted with scenes from the Stations of the Cross.

Sometimes even the crowds up here can get to you, and weekends are best avoided if you have an aversion to queues. Once you've had enough, follow the old fortifications southeast and head

DON'T MISS

- walking along the Hunger Wall (5, C6)
- relaxing in the rose garden
- stopping to take in city views
- taking a peek through the telescope at the Štefánik Observatory

through the crumbling stone Hunger Wall to the southern side of the hill. Here in peaceful **Kinský Gardens** you'll find lots of places to relax, and not too far in is the unique construction of the **Church of St Michael**.

The once imposing Hunger Wall is dwarfed by Petřín Tower

STRAHOV MONASTERY (2, B3)

The giant white **Strahov Monastery** (Strahovský Klášter) looks down from its Petřín Hill vantage point over the most dense part of Malá Strana, a serene view that gives its grounds an extra-meditative quality. The imposing monastery was established in 1140 by Prince Vladislav II for the Premonstratensians, followers of the teachings of St Augustine, but the complex didn't undergo its most significant developments (including the reconstruction of a brewery) until the 17th and 18th centuries.

The highlight of a visit to Strahov, apart from the inherent pleasure in just getting to its delightful location, is its **library**, comprising one of the oldest monastic collections in the country. Researchers get access to many of the priceless books and manuscripts. Others have to be content with glimpses of the 50,000 tomes housed in the baroque, double-storey **Philosophy Hall**, built in 1794 and decorated with a fresco by Anton Maulbertsch, and the 16,000 books in the equally stunning **Theology Hall**. The **Strahov Gallery** (p30) has a collection of monastic paintings and sculptures from Bohemia and elsewhere in Europe.

If you've yet to have your fill of weighty baroque, have a look at the interior of the **Church of the Assumption of Our Lady**, built in 1143.

INFORMATION

- ☎ library 220 516 671, museum 224 511 137
- ✉ Strahovské nádvoří 1, Strahov
- € library 70/50Kč, museum 30/15Kč
- ☽ library 9am–noon & 1-5pm, museum 9am-5pm Tue-Sun
- ⓘ library viewed by tour only
- Ⓜ Malostranská, then tram 22 or 23 to Pohořelec
- ✕ Klášterní Pivovar Strahov (p67)

Enjoy the serenity of Strahov Monastery

There's also a **Museum of Czech Literature** here, though the inherently interesting assorted manuscripts and temporary exhibitions don't make a lot of sense unless you can read Czech.

DON'T MISS

- the 9th-century jewel-encrusted Strahov gospel
- the *xyloteka* (books bound in the bark of the trees they describe)
- the preserved sea creatures in the 'Cabinet of Curiosities'

MUSEUM OF DECORATIVE ARTS (4, C2)

Established in 1898 to celebrate Emperor Franz Josef's Golden Jubilee, the **Museum of Decorative Arts** (Umčlecko-Průmyslové Muzeum) opened in 1900 as part of a pan-European movement to encourage a return to the old craftsmanship and aestheticism that had been sacrificed to the mass-production ethic of the Industrial Revolution. It hosts an exemplary display of 16th- to early-20th-century artistry, and has now amassed over 250,000 artefacts, though you'll find only a fraction of these on display here at any one time.

Above reception is a hall for temporary exhibitions, which are often well worth a look; they usually showcase works by young contemporary designers, artists and photographers. But the main reason for visiting is the permanent top-floor exhibit called the **Story of Materials**. Here you'll find wonderful displays of glass, Meissen and Wedgewood porcelain, Italian majolica, Art Nouveau pewter, silver, tapestries and timepieces, including a chunky cubist clock by Josef Gočár. There's also an exhibition of women's fashions, from the kind of prim early-1800s smocks that Jane Austen might have worn, to garish 1960s and '70s outfits, while on the level above that there's a collection of ecclesiastical garments dating back as far as the 14th century.

A small number of early books, prints, posters and baroque and cubist furniture complete the small but fascinating displays. An integral part of the museum's magnificent horde of jewels is on show at the **Prague Jewellery Collection** (p28).

> ## DON'T MISS
> • the collection of Art Nouveau advertising posters
> • glass figurines of footballers and sea creatures by Jaroslav Brychta
> • stunning desks by Josef Danhauser and Josef Gočár
> • the stairwell ceiling and stained-glass windows

INFORMATION
- ☎ 251 093 265
- 🖥 www.upm.cz
- ✉ 17.listopadu 2, Josefov
- € Story of Materials & temporary exhibition 120/60Kč, temporary exhibition only 80Kč, children up to 10 free
- 🕐 10am-8pm Tue, 10am-6pm Wed-Sun
- ⓘ free audio guides
- Ⓜ Staroměstská
- ♿ good
- 🍴 on-site café

MUSEUM OF THE CITY OF PRAGUE (4, J2)

The rich history of the Czech capital is laid out before you at the **Museum of the City of Prague** (Muzeum Hlavního Města Prahy). The slightly out-of-the-way location means it sees far fewer visitors than it deserves, but at least you won't have to elbow your way through the crowds to appreciate the museum and its many treasures.

The first gallery, unfortunately the only one without English labelling, displays archaeological finds, including stone tools and pottery. You can pick up a free guide in foreign languages at the cash desk. Next comes the medieval exhibition, where highlights include a 14th-century wooden *Pietà* and Hussite flails and clubs.

INFORMATION

☎ 224 816 772
🖥 www.muzeumprahy.cz
✉ Na Poříčí 52, Nové Město
ℹ 9am-6pm Tue-Sun
Ⓜ Florenc
✗ U Rozvařilů (p74)

DON'T MISS

- Antonio Sacchetti's panorama of Prague around the stairwell
- the Prague Brewers' Guild drum
- the armoured Sign of the Iron Man
- life-size wooden angels by Jan Jiří Bendl

The detail is astronomical

Renaissance guild signs, ecclesiastical chalices, porcelain and more weapons grace the upper floor. Don't miss the haunting 18th-century painted panel that tells, in strip-cartoon form, the tragic and gruesome tale of Simon Abeles, a Jewish boy apparently murdered by his father and uncle in 1694 for converting to Christianity. Simon was buried with pomp at the Church of Our Lady Before Týn, while his father hanged himself and his uncle was publicly tortured to death. This pretty panel once hung in a church.

The Astronomical Clock's original 1866 calendar wheel, painted by Josef Mánes, is here too, but the museum's star turn is the amazing 1:480 scale model of Prague, created by Antonín Langweil between 1826 and 1837. The attention to detail is breathtaking, with every stone and every window of more than 2000 buildings accurately reproduced. It's an invaluable historical record of the city at that time and a must-see for any visitor to Prague. Temporary exhibitions fill the remaining halls.

CHURCH OF OUR LADY BEFORE TÝN (7, D2)

Rising up behind the Týnská School (a parish school until the mid-19th century) is the hallowed mass of the **Church of Our Lady Before Týn** (Kostel Panny Marie Před Týnem), its exterior bristling with dramatic Gothic touches – the north portal is topped by a 14th-century tympanum. The cathedral is an Old Town Square landmark with distinctive twin spires that are a reassuring sight to many tourists after losing their bearings in the narrow surrounding byways

Construction on the Týn church began in 1380 to replace another chapel, but the building contract apparently didn't specify an end date, and subsequent years saw the completion of items such as the roof (1457), gable (1463), southern tower (1511) and a new northern tower (1835).

The church was initially one of the strongholds of Hussitism, the church-reform movement championed by Jan Hus in the late 14th and early 15th centuries, but eventually succumbed to Catholicism and the lavish worship of baroque interior design.

INFORMATION

- ✉ Staroměstské náměstí, Staré Město
- € free
- 🕐 services at 12.15pm Mon-Fri, 8am Sat, 9.30am & 9pm Sun; official sightseeing 9am-noon & 1-2pm Mon-Fri
- ℹ occasional concerts
- Ⓜ Staroměstská or Můstek
- ♿ good (entry from Celetná)
- 🍴 Rybí trh (p78)

Týnská School in Old Town Square

The focus of the massive interior of the Church of Our Lady Before Týn is its ornate altar (1649), erected to give thanks after the invading Swedes were repulsed, while the ceiling is decorated with colourful heraldic shields from Habsburg times. The astronomer Tycho Brahe was buried here; apparently, he died when his bladder burst during a mammoth drinking bout in 1601.

The Church entrance is at the far end of the passageway that opens up beside the House at the Stone Bell (p29) on the Old Town Square, although opening hours for sightseeing visits are erratic, and the church is normally only open for services.

DON'T MISS

- the tomb of Tycho Brahe
- the ornate 15th-century pulpit
- the sound of the renovated 17th-century pipe organ during concerts (see p82)

VYŠEHRAD (6, C5)

Sometimes referred to as 'Prague's second castle', **Vyšehrad** (just *hrad* to Czechs) today is more of a pleasant walled park, especially popular with local families on the weekends, than the forbidding fortress it once was. According to legend, the first castle was raised here in the 7th century by the Slavonic chieftain Krok, whose daughter, Libuše, later founded Prague itself

In the late 11th century, King Vratislav II chose Vyšehrad as the site for a palace, the **Church of Sts Peter & Paul**, and what is now the city's oldest Romanesque structure, **St Martin Rotunda**. However, the subsequent rise of Prague Castle as the royal seat meant the decline of this southern stronghold. Charles IV resurrected Vyšehrad with a Gothic palace, but it was badly damaged during the Hussite wars. After a stint as an army garrison, the fortress attracted attention from 19th-century Romantic artists and nationalists; Smetana set his opera *Libuše* here. The castle has had four major reconstructions.

The vibrant interior of the church is a surprisingly harmonious mixture of neo-Gothic, baroque and, most strikingly, Art Nouveau, with stylish frescoes of saints and swirling botanical-inspired motifs by František and Marie Urban covering the walls. The **Chapel of the Holy Sacrament** is adorned with frescoes by the Viennese artist Karl Jobst. Of special significance to Czechs is **Vyšehrad Cemetery**, containing the tombs of Dvořák, Smetana and Jan Neruda.

INFORMATION

- ✉ Soběslavova 2, Vyšehrad
- € grounds free, Church of Sts Peter & Paul 20/10Kč
- ☾ grounds open 24hr; church 9am-noon & 1-5pm Mon, Wed, Thu & Sat, 9am-noon Fri, 11am-noon & 1-5pm Sun, closed Tue
- ⓘ information centre (open 9.30am-6pm) just beyond Tábor Gate, approached from the metro station
- Ⓜ Vyšehrad
- ♿ good
- ✗ U Vyšehradské Rotundy (p80)

STUFF OF LEGENDS

Czech legends attempt to explain the birth of Prague in mythological terms, most (it's been theorised) constructed in the minds of social chroniclers. Vyšehrad features heavily in these stories, and this legendary status has made the old fortress a magnet for poets, painters and composers, particularly those who were working during the 19th-century resurgence of Czech culture (Czech National Revival) and sought an enigmatic icon to represent the country's past.

LORETA (2, B2)

The **Loreta** is an elaborate pilgrimage site established by Baroness Benigna Katharina von Lobkowicz in 1626, and subsequently maintained and protected by the Capuchins, an order associated with St Francis of Assisi's brotherhood. At the heart of the complex is a replica of the **Santa Casa**, the Virgin Mary's alleged house, which stood in Nazareth before being dismantled by pilgrims and shipped to Loreto in Italy in 1294. Legend has it that angels provided the transportation, but this could have something to do with the name of the family that patronised the house-moving: Angeli.

The Santa Casa copy is an over-decorated baroque cube, which has fragmentary frescoes inside, and houses the wonder-working statue (its actual name) of **Our Lady of Loreto**. Around the courtyard run frescoed cloisters. The **Church of the Nativity of Our Lord** has a deliriously baroque altar, a rococo organ and some beautiful frescoes; the side altars of Sts Felicissimus and Marcia contain the aristocratically dressed remains of two Spanish martyrs. In the southwestern corner is the **Chapel of Our Lady of Sorrows**, which has a sculpture of a crucified bearded woman. Apparently St Starosta successfully prayed for a beard to maintain her chastity, but her father had her crucified for thus derailing her arranged marriage. She is the patron saint of the needy and godforsaken.

DON'T MISS
- the 'Prague Sun' monstrance and its 6000-plus diamonds in the Treasury
- the 27-bell carillon at entrance played on the hour
- the *Presentation in the Temple* fresco in the Church of the Nativity of Our Lord

Tours end with the **Treasury** and its glittery display of chalices, crosses and monstrances donated by pilgrims and patrons. Note that photography is strictly forbidden anywhere in the Loreta.

INFORMATION
- ☎ 220 516 740
- ✉ Loretánské náměstí 7, Hradčany
- € 90/70Kč
- 🕙 9am-12.15pm & 1-4.30pm Tue-Sun; services at 7.30am Sat, 6pm Sun
- Ⓜ Malostranská, then tram 22 or 23 to Pohořelec
- 🍴 Malý Buddha (p67)

ST NICHOLAS CHURCH (5, C3)

There are three churches called St Nicholas in Prague, but only one that took 82 years and three generations of one family to build, and is regarded as an outstanding example of baroque architecture. This is the **St Nicholas Church** (Kostel Sv Mikuláše) that's located west of the Vltava and has greedily consumed most of the available space in Malostranské náměstí, dominating the local skyline with its 70m-high verdigris dome. Work on the church was started by a Jesuit order in 1673, but it was a Dientzenhofer father-son act, plus a next-generation son-in-law, who were directly responsible for the construction of the church, which was finally finished in 1755.

INFORMATION

- ✉ Malostranské náměstí 38, Malá Strana
- € 50/25Kč, belfry 40/30Kč
- ⏱ 8.30am-4.45pm, belfry 10am-6pm
- ℹ concerts usually at 6pm
- Ⓜ Malostranská, then tram 12, 22, 23 or 57
- ✕ U tří Zlatých Hvězd (p71)

The incredible late-baroque interior is awash with gilt and marble, and contains numerous pillars, frescoes and dramatically gesturing over-life-size statues of saints. One of the artists who had a hand in the 10 years' worth of interior decorating was Karel Škréta, who produced a painting for the chapel's main altar. Mozart ran his fingers over the 2500-pipe organ in 1787, and was honoured with a Requiem mass here after his death. If you're not feeling too giddy from the ornamentation, you can also climb the bell tower for an extra fee.

ART IMITATES ROOF

The enormous ceiling fresco, *Apotheosis of St Nicholas*, by Johann Lucas Kracker, is the largest in Europe. To check out its other claim to fame, head up to the gallery and look at how the painting has been skilfully rendered to blend near-perfectly with the ceiling architecture, so the two are practically inseparable.

It's baroque around the clock

Sights & Activities

MUSEUMS

Army Museum (6, D4-E4)
The grim barrack-like building that houses this museum has seen better days, but the extensive collection of WWI and WWII uniforms, weapons, battle dioramas and other Czech and foreign militaria are worth a look. There are regular temporary exhibitions but labelling is Czech only throughout.
☎ 973 204 924 ⌧ U Památníku 2, Žižkov € free 🕑 9.30am-6pm Tue-Sun Ⓜ Florenc

Ceremonial Hall (4, C2)
Formerly the Old Jewish Cemetery mortuary and now part of the Jewish Museum (p12), the Ceremonial Hall (Obřadní Síň), built in 1912, is the site of an interesting exhibition on Jewish traditions relating to illness and death.
☎ 222 317 191 🖳 www .jewishmuseum.cz ⌧ U starého hřbitova 3a, Josefov € Jewish Museum 300/200Kč 🕑 9am-4.30pm Sun-Fri Nov-Mar, 9am-6pm Sun-Fri Apr-Oct, closed Jewish holidays Ⓜ Staroměstská

Jewish traditions on display

Czech Museum of Fine Arts (7, B3)
This easily overlooked little gallery, on the corner of Karlova and Husova, is an exhibition space for rotating displays of modern art. The cellar usually houses sculptures, while the upper two floors display paintings and installations.
☎ 222 220 418 ⌧ Husova 19-21, Staré Město € 50/20Kč 🕑 10am-6pm Tue-Sun Ⓜ Staroměstská

Czech Museum of Music (5, C4)
This absorbing museum displays several orchestras' worth of musical instruments, from grand pianos and harpsichords to trombones, tubas and hurdy-gurdies. Listening posts in every room play recordings of the often very rare instruments; discover why the quarter-tone piano never caught on. Concerts are sporadically held downstairs.
☎ 257 327 285 🖳 www .nm.cz ⌧ Karmelitská 2, Malá Strana € 100/50Kč 🕑 10am-6pm Tue-Sun Ⓜ Malostranská, then tram 12, 22, 23 or 57 to Hellichova ♿ good

Dvořák Museum (6, D5)
Lodged in the baroque Villa Amerika, built in 1720, the Dvořák Museum displays a dry collection of photos, letters and personal belongings of the great composer, including his piano, monogrammed hankies and honorary graduation gown from Cambridge. This is for real fans only. The upstairs frescoed salon hosts occasional concerts.

☎ 224 923 363 🖳 www .nm.cz ⌧ Ke Karlovu 20, Nové Město € 70/40Kč 🕑 10am-1.30pm & 2-5.30pm Tue-Sun Ⓜ IP Pavlova

Franz Kafka Museum (4, B3)
Learn about Prague's literary hero at this impressively staged exhibition. Peruse Kafka's rarely cheery letters, then shuffle through the 'Endless Office', a claustrophobic space filled with filing cabinets, flickering video screens and the sounds of ringing telephones. At the end is a surreal video installation inspired by *The Castle*.
☎ 221 451 333 🖳 www .kafkamuseum.cz ⌧ Cihelná 2b, Malá Strana € 120/60Kč 🕑 10am-6pm Tue-Sun Ⓜ Malostranská

Lapidárium (6, D2)
Quality examples of the mason's art gather in this gallery of Bohemian sculpture. Highlights include the Kouřim Lions (the country's oldest stone sculpture), Jan Bendl's original equestrian statue of St Wenceslas, the flamboyant Renaissance Krocín Fountain and several Charles Bridge statues. The stately bronzes of Habsburg emperors and Marshal Radecký look forlorn in the last room.
☎ 233 375 636 🖳 www .nm.cz ⌧ Fairgrounds (U Výstaviště 422), Holešovice € 40/20Kč 🕑 noon-6pm Tue-Fri, 10am-6pm Sat & Sun Ⓜ Nádraží Holešovice, then tram 5, 12, 17, 53 or 54 to U Výstaviště ♿ good

Lobkowicz Palace (8, F1)
The Lobkovický palác contains the National Museum

SOMETHING FOR NOTHING

A healthy number of museums and galleries in Prague prescribe to the idea of public days, where entry fees are waived or reduced to a token amount. All National Gallery branches hold their open day on the first Wednesday of every month, and the National Museum and associated City of Prague museum have theirs on the first Monday and Thursday of each month, respectively. Freebies are noted in the relevant reviews. Children between six and 10 years of age often gain free admittance to exhibitions.

exposition 'Monuments of the National Past', covering Czech history from earliest times to the attempted democratic revolution of 1848. Eclectic exhibits include the moustachioed stone head of a Celtic god and Napoleon's wine glass. The extensive notes will guide you through it all.
☎ 233 354 467 🖳 www .nm.cz ✉ Jiřská 3, Prague Castle, Hradčany € 40/20Kč ☾ 9am-5pm Tue-Sun Ⓜ Malostranská, then tram 22 or 23 to Pražskýhrad ♿ limited

Mucha Museum (4, F4)
See the fine works of Art Nouveau master Alfons Mucha up close and personal. On show are some of his original theatrical posters, as well as his *Slav Epic* paintings and popular commercial posters such as *The Four Flowers*. Don't miss the photographs of Mucha's truly bohemian models and friends, including a trouserless Paul Gauguin.
☎ 221 451 333 🖳 www .mucha.cz ✉ Panská 7, Nové Město € 120/60Kč ☾ 10am-6pm Ⓜ Můstek ♿ good

Old Royal Palace (8, D2)
Dating from 1135, the centrepiece of this grand Gothic palace is the huge, vaulted Vladislav Hall; the balcony presents an awesome vista over Prague. Off to one side is the Bohemian chancellery, where the infamous Second Defenestration of Prague took place in 1618; the lucky defenestrates actually survived after landing in a vast pile of refuse.
☎ 224 373 368 ✉ Prague Castle, Hradčany € see p8 for admission prices ☾ 9am-5pm Apr-Oct, 9am-4pm Nov-Mar Ⓜ Malostranská, then tram 22 or 23 to Pražskýhrad ♿ Vladislav Hall only

Old Town Hall (7, C2)
Founded in 1338, the Old Town Hall (Staroměstská Radnice) is a medieval complex presided over by the Gothic tower with its Astronomical Clock (p10). On the 1st floor is the Gothic Chapel, though most visitors head straight for the 60m tower, with great views over the square. Halls on the ground floor display temporary exhibitions.

☎ 12 444 ✉ Staroměstské náměstí 1, Staré Město € 50/40Kč, tower 40/30Kč ☾ 11am-6pm Mon, 9am-6pm Tue-Sun Apr-Oct, 11am-5pm Mon, 9am-5pm Tue-Sun Nov-Mar Ⓜ Staroměstská ♿ good

Podskalí Customs House (6, C5)
The sole remnant of the once bustling riverside community of Podskalí, this 16th-century Customs House (now sunk below present ground level) controlled the lucrative timber trade on the Vltava. Upstairs, the small museum recalls the area's commercial heyday with photographs and models. There's a traditional restaurant downstairs (p74).
☎ 224 919 833 ✉ Rašínovo nábřeží 412, Nové Město € 30/20Kč ☾ 10am-6pm Tue-Sun Ⓜ Karlovo Náměstí, then tram 3, 7, 16, 17 or 21 to Svobodova

Prague Castle Powder Tower (2, B3)
Edward Kelly and other alchemists sweated over their furnaces in this forbidding tower, also known as the Mihulka Tower, vainly attempting to produce gold for Emperor Rudolf II (see p33). It was later used as a gunpowder store and today presents a small display on the history of the Prague Castle Guards.
☎ 224 373 368 ✉ Prague Castle, Hradčany € see p8 for admission prices ☾ 9am-5pm Apr-Oct, 9am-4pm Nov-Mar Ⓜ Malostranská, then tram 22 or 23 to Pražskýhrad

Prague Jewellery Collection (4, B3)

Sumptuous necklaces, brooches, bangles and rings from the collections of the Museum of Decorative Arts (p20) are shown here, including some eye-catching baubles by the likes of Tiffany and Fabergé. Vintage evening gowns and exhibitions of contemporary Czech designers complete the collection.

☎ 221 451 333 ✉ Cihelná 2b, Malá Strana € 60/50Kč ⏱ 10am-6pm Ⓜ Malostranská

The Story of Prague Castle (8, D2)

This superb exhibition fills the extensive Gothic halls below the Old Royal Palace (p27). Armour belonging to St Wenceslas, the raffish and remarkably well-preserved clothes in which Emperor Rudolf II was entombed in 1612, and clothes, crowns and regalia removed from the tombs of other Czech rulers are on display, plus archaeological finds from the castle site.

☎ 224 373 368 ✉ Prague Castle, Hradčany € see p8 for admission prices

⏱ 9am-5pm Apr-Oct, 9am-4pm Nov-Mar Ⓜ Malostranská, then tram 22 or 23 to Pražskýhrad

GALLERIES

Convent of St Agnes (4, E1)

Upstairs in this 13th-century convent (Klášter Sv Anežky) is the National Gallery's exhibition of Bohemian and Central European medieval art, including multiple Madonnas, Bohemia's oldest preserved panel painting (c 1340) and the immense Velhartice Altarpiece (c 1500). Also here are portraits of saints, commissioned by Charles IV for Karlštejn Castle (p48).

☎ 224 810 628 🖥 www .ngprague.cz ✉ Anežská 1, Josefov € 100/50Kč, 2-day ticket incl Convent of St George & Sternberg Palace 240/120Kč, free 1st Wed of month ⏱ 10am-6pm Tue-Sun Ⓜ Náměstí Republiky, then tram 5, 8, 14 or 53 ♿ limited

Convent of St George (8, D1)

This former Benedictine convent (Klášter Sv Jiří) presents an exhibition of 'Mannerist

and Baroque Art in Bohemia', featuring artists such as Karel Škréta and Petr Brandl. The flamboyant religious paintings and statuary are interesting enough, but soon become monotonous.

☎ 257 320 536 🖥 www .ngprague.cz ✉ Jiřské náměstí 33, Prague Castle, Hradčany € see p8 for admission prices ⏱ 9am-5pm Apr-Oct, 9am-4pm Nov-Mar Ⓜ Malostranská, then tram 22 or 23 to Pražskýhrad

House at the Golden Ring (7, D2)

Much of the Renaissance Dům U zlatého prstenu is taken up by a fascinating exhibition of 20th-century art, with particular emphasis on the Czech passion for surrealism and just plain oddness. Standouts include Jan Zrzavý's bleak *Slagheaps in the Evening*, *A Bird Above* by Emil Filla, and Karel Malich's creepy wire sculpture, *Would You Like Another Beer?*

☎ 224 827 022 🖥 www .citygallery prague.cz ✉ Týnská 6, Staré Město € 90/50Kč ⏱ 10am-6pm Tue-Sun Ⓜ Náměstí Republiky ♿ limited

MUCH ADO ABOUT MUCHA

The Mucha Museum does a great job of presenting the life and times of Alfons Mucha, aided by the cooperation it receives from the celebrated artist's grandson and daughter-in-law in the guise of the Mucha Foundation. In fact, Mucha has become a very marketable commodity, as evidenced by the countless postcards, calendars, posters, mugs, playing cards, fridge magnets and other touristy knick-knackery you'll see all around town. To appreciate some of his greatest work, take a tour of the Municipal House (p15).

House at the Stone Bell (7, C2-D2)

Dating from the 14th century, this carefully restored Gothic building (Dům U Kamenného Zvonu) overlooking Old Town Square is another branch of the Prague City Gallery. It hosts temporary art exhibitions throughout the year. ☎ 224 827 526 🖳 www .citygalleryprague.cz ✉ Staroměstské náměstí 13, Staré Město € 100/70Kč 🕑 10am-6pm Tue-Sun Ⓜ Náměstí Republiky ♿ limited

Kampa Museum (4, A4)

This gallery, in a renovated mill complex, is devoted to 'modern central European art', based around a large collection of abstract works by František Kupka. There are cubist bronzes by Otto Gutfreund and pieces by contemporary artists from Poland, Hungary and elsewhere. ☎ 257 286 147 🖳 www .muzeumkampa.cz ✉ U sovových mlýnů 2, Malá Strana € 120/60Kč 🕑 10am-6pm 🚊 tram 6, 9, 22, 23, 57 or 58

Kinský Palace (7, D2)

It was from the balcony of the rococo Palác Kinských that Klement Gottwald proclaimed communist rule in 1948. The National Gallery now keeps its collection of 20th-century Czech landscape paintings here, and it's also used as a temporary exhibition space. ☎ 224 810 758 🖳 www.ng prague.cz ✉ Staroměstské náměstí 12, Staré Město € 100/50Kč, free 1st Wed of month 🕑 10am-6pm Tue-Sun Ⓜ Staroměstská, Můstek ♿ limited

Kinský Palace was built between 1755 and 1765

Mánes Gallery (6, C4)

Built in 1930 for the Mánes Visual Artists Association, and considered a masterpiece of 'functionalist' architecture, this gallery remains a leading exhibition hall for rotating displays by contemporary Czech artists. The adjoining water tower, dating from 1495, was part of a medieval mill that once stood here. ☎ 224 930 754 🖳 www .galeriemanes.cz ✉ Masarykovo nábřeží 250, Nové Město € 40/20Kč 🕑 10am-6pm Tue-Sun Ⓜ Karlovo Náměstí ♿ good

Prague Castle Gallery (8, B2)

Occupying the former castle stables, this gallery exhibits the small but impressive art collection begun by the Habsburg emperors. Works by Titian, Tintoretto, Lucas Cranach the Elder and Veronese adorn the walls,

as well as a gigantic, and rather overcrowded canvas by Rubens, *Assembly of the Gods at Olympus*. ☎ 224 373 368 ✉ Prague Castle, Hradčany € 100/ 50Kč 🕑 10am-6pm Ⓜ Malostranská, then tram 22 or 23 to Pražskýhrad ♿ good

Robert Guttmann Gallery (4, D2)

Part of the Jewish Museum (p12), this small gallery, named in honour of the early-20th-century Prague artist, opened in 2001 and hosts temporary art exhibitions on Jewish themes. ☎ 221 711 511 🖳 www .jewishmuseum.cz ✉ U Staré školy 3, Josefov € 30/15Kč, incl Jewish Museum 300/200Kč 🕑 10am-4.30pm Sun-Fri Nov-Mar, 10am-6pm Sun-Fri Apr-Oct, closed Jewish holidays Ⓜ Staroměstská

Sternberg Palace (2, C1)

Accessed by a passageway next to Archbishop's Palace, the baroque Šternberský palác serves as a branch of the National Gallery and has a remarkable collection of Old Masters, including works by El Greco, Piero della Francesca, Rembrandt and Rubens. Roman and Renaissance sculptures are also on show.
☎ 220 514 599 ☐ www .ngprague.cz ✉ Hradčanské náměstí 15, Hradčany € 150/70Kč, 2-day ticket incl Convent of St Agnes & Convent of St George 240/120Kč, free 1st Wed of month ☼ 10am-6pm Tue-Sun Ⓜ Malostranská ♿ ground floor only

Strahov Gallery (2, B3)

This important monastic art collection displays works from the 14th to the 19th centuries, with awe-inspiring exhibits such as the naturalistic *Crucifix of Jihlava* (1340) and the *Strahov Madonna* from the same period. The ticket includes the cloisters downstairs – don't miss the Winter Refectory with its extraordinary trompe l'oeil ceiling fresco of a merry banqueting scene.
☎ 220 517 278 ☐ www .strahovmonastery.cz ✉ Strahovské nádvoří 1, Strahov € 50/20Kč ☼ 9am-noon & 12.30-5pm Tue-Sun Ⓜ Malostranská, then tram 22 or 23 to Pohořelec

Summer Palace (5, C1)

The 16th-century Královský Leto hrádek is a particularly fine example of Italian Renaissance architecture. Often referred to as the 'Belvedere', it stages temporary art exhibitions during the summer.
☎ 220 612 230 ✉ Prague Castle, Hradčany ☼ 10am-6pm Tue-Sun May-Sep, 10am-5pm Tue-Sun Apr & Oct Ⓜ Malostranská, then tram 22 or 23 to Pražskýhrad ♿ ground floor only

Troja Chateau (6, C1)

This fabulous baroque palace, straight opposite the Prague zoo (p42), presides over a huge and equally grand formal garden. Inside is an exhibition of 19th-century Czech paintings and 20th-century sculpture, and original frescoes glorifying the Habsburg dynasty adorn the walls and ceilings.
☎ 283 851 614 ✉ U Trojského zámku 1, Troja € 140/70Kč, grounds free ☼ 10am-6pm Tue-Sun Ⓜ Nádraží Holešovice, then bus 112 to Zoo Praha ♿ grounds

NOTABLE BUILDINGS & MONUMENTS

Adria Palace (4, E5)

This gigantic imitation Venetian palace was built in the 1920s, in a bulky, short-lived style known as 'rondocubism', for the Adriatica Insurance Company. Seek out the elaborate 24-hour clock surrounded by bronze statuettes, representing the signs of the zodiac, in the open foyer.
✉ cnr Národní třída & Jungmannova, Nové Město Ⓜ Národní Třída ♿ good

Dancing Building (6, C4-C5)

Completed in 1996 by architects Vlado Miluníc and Frank Gehry, the Dancing Building (Tančící dům), with its graceful, fluid form, blends remarkably well with its older neighbours. The slim-waisted glass tower hugging its more upright partner does look like a pair of dancers, hence the name. One of Prague's best restaurants, La Perle de Prague (p73), occupies the 7th floor.
✉ Rašínovo nábřeží 80, Nové Město Ⓜ Karlovo Náměstí

Stepping out at the Sternberg Palace

The graceful yet fluid Dancing Building

Estates Theatre (7, D3)

Prague's oldest concert hall opened as the Nostitz Theatre in 1783, and Mozart conducted the premiere of his opera *Don Giovanni* here in 1787. Later renamed after the collective Bohemian nobility, the Stavovské Divadlo is now a principal Prague venue for operas, concerts and ballets, including the annual Opera Mozart festival.

☎ 224 215 001 🖳 www .narodni-divadlo.cz
✉ Ovocný trh 1, Staré Město
🕐 box office (Kolowrat Palace) 10am-6pm Mon-Fri, 10am-12.30pm & 3-6pm Sat & Sun Ⓜ Můstek ♿ good

František Palacký Monument (6, C5)

Stanislav Sucharda's bronze tribute to the 19th-century historian and leading figure of the Czech National Revival

(p104) is a wild affair. The writer sits, unperturbed, amid a swarm of fantastical Art Nouveauish creatures including winged, half-human gargoyles and what looks like an insensible naked woman stretched out at the back. Only in Prague.
✉ Palackého náměstí, Nové Město Ⓜ Karlovo Náměstí ♿ good

Franz Kafka Statue (4, D2)

One of Prague's latest landmarks, Jaroslav Rona's bronze tribute to Kafka outside the Spanish Synagogue depicts the writer sitting on the shoulders of a giant, striding empty suit; the image was inspired by Kafka's story *Description of a Struggle*.
✉ cnr Dušní & Vězeňská, Josefov Ⓜ Staroměstská ♿ excellent

Jan Hus Statue (7, C2)

Diverting pedestrian traffic in the middle of Old Town Square is the commanding presence of Jan Hus, erected on 6 July 1915, the 500th anniversary of the reformer's execution. The sombreness of Ladislav Šaloun's statue, which casts Hus alongside his followers and a mother and child representing a reborn Czech nation, is relieved a little by encircling flowerbeds.
✉ Staroměstské náměstí, Staré Město Ⓜ Staroměstská ♿ excellent

Klementinum (7, A3)

The massive Klementinum was a Jesuit college before becoming part of Charles University in 1773. From the inner courtyard, catch a tour of the grand baroque library – note that the tomes are off-limits – and the 52m-high reconstructed Astronomical Tower.
☎ 603 231 241 ✉ Marián-ské náměstí, Staré Město
€ 100/50Kč 🕐 noon-7pm Mon-Fri, 10am-7pm Sat & Sun Ⓜ Staroměstská
♿ library only

Memorial to the Victims of Communism (5, C6)

Unveiled in 2002 as a memorial to the victims of communist regimes across the world, this dramatic monument consists of a flight of big concrete steps leading up from Újezd, topped with a series of increasingly fragmentary bronze statues of a naked man, designed by sculptor Olbram Zoubek.
✉ Újezd, Malá Strana Ⓜ Malostranská ♿ good

OPERATION ANTHROPOID

One of the most daring and dangerous missions of WWII was Operation Anthropoid, the plan to 'liquidate' the brutal Nazi Reichsprotektor of Bohemia and Moravia, Reinhard Heydrich. British-trained Czechoslovak parachutists were dropped inside Czechoslovakia in December 1941 and on 27 May 1942 they ambushed Heydrich's staff car in the Libeň area of Prague. Heydrich died of his wounds in hospital, and a huge reward was offered for information on his killers. On 10 June Nazi fury was directed at the village of Lidice 18km northwest of Prague, which they completely destroyed, while on 18 June the seven parachutists' hiding place in the Cathedral of Sts Cyril & Methodius (opposite) was betrayed. Eight hundred German soldiers surrounded the building, but after a fierce gun fight, the parachutists shot themselves rather than be taken alive. The crypt is today kept as a shrine to their memory.

Old Jewish Cemetery
(7, B1)

With some 12,000 ancient, cascading tombstones, this atmospheric cemetery (Starý Zidovský Hřbitov) established in the 15th century is now part of the Jewish Museum (p12). Among the dignitaries buried here is Rabbi Loew (see p12). His elaborate tomb is a site of pilgrimage, often covered with coins and candles.
☎ 222 317 191 ⌨ www .jewishmuseum.cz ✉ Široká, Josefov € incl Jewish Museum 300/200Kč ⏰ 9am-4.30pm Sun-Fri Nov-Mar, 9am-6pm Sun-Fri Apr-Oct, closed Jewish holidays Ⓜ Staroměstská ♿ good

Old Town Bridge Tower
(4, C4)

The striking 14th-century Staroměstská mostecká věž was the point where invading Swedes were repulsed in 1648 by a force of Catholic students and Jews. Today it houses a fairly humdrum collection of vintage musical instruments. The main point of interest is the 138-step climb to the roof, for amazing views across the river.
✉ Karlův most, Staré Město € 50/40Kč ⏰ 10am-6pm Ⓜ Staroměstská

Powder Tower (7, F2)

There are fine views from this 65m-high neo-Gothic tower (Prašná Brána), built in 1475 and used to store gunpowder in the 18th century. It now has an appropriately sooty look and a photo exhibit on the Prague skyline. Be careful on the steep stairs up to the 1st-floor ticket office.
✉ Na příkopě, Staré Město € 40/30Kč ⏰ 10am-6pm (last entry 5.30pm) Apr-Oct Ⓜ Náměstí Republiky

TV Tower (6, E4)

This 216m tower (Televizní Věž) is the tallest, and possibly the ugliest thing in Prague. On a clear day you can see up to 100km away from the viewing deck. The exterior is graced by a series of giant babies with barcodes for faces, created by artist David Černý.
☎ 267 005 778 ⌨ www .tower.cz ✉ Mahlerovy sady 1, Žižkov € 150/30Kč ⏰ 11am-11.30pm Ⓜ Jiřího z Poděbrad

PLACES OF WORSHIP

Basilica of St George
(8, D2)

Founded in AD 920 by Duke Vratislav I, Bazilika Sv Jiří is the best-preserved Romanesque church in the country. The façade, though, is baroque, and the place was heavily restored in the 19th century. There are remnants of frescoes, and the chapels of St Ludmila and St John of Nepomuk are splendid.
☎ info centre 224 373 368 ✉ Prague Castle, Hradčany € see p8 for admission prices ⏰ 9am-5pm Apr-Oct, 9am-4pm Nov-Mar Ⓜ Malostranská, then tram 22 or 23 to Pražskýhrad

Bethlehem Chapel (4, D4)

A treasured national icon, this little church was built in 1391 as a venue for Czech-language sermons, and the most famous of the preachers here was the great reformer, Jan Hus. Unfortunately, it was demolished in the 18th century; what you see today was rebuilt in the early

1950s, incorporating some original elements.
✉ Betlémské náměstí 3, Staré Město € 35/20Kč ☉ 10am-6.30pm Tue-Sun Apr-Oct, 11am-5.30pm Nov-Mar 🚊 tram 17, 18, 51 or 54

Cathedral of Sts Cyril & Methodius (6, C4)

This baroque Orthodox church is where the para-chutists involved in Operation Anthropoid (see opposite) hid out and died, after it was stormed by Nazi troops. The crypt now houses the moving 'Memorial to the Heroes of the Heydrich Terror'.
☎ 224 916 100
✉ Resslova, Nové Město
€ 50/20Kč ☉ 10am-5pm Tue-Sun Ⓜ Karlovo Náměstí
♿ good

Church of Our Lady of the Snows (4, E5)

Though planned on a grand scale in the 14th century, only the chancel of the Kostel Panny Marie Sněžné was ever completed, accounting for its odd proportions: it seems taller than it is long, while its towering black and gold altar is the city's

The striking baroque Church of our Lady of the Snows

highest. The front courtyard is accessed through the archway of the Austrian Cultural Institute.
✉ Jungmannovo náměstí 18, Nové Město ☉ 6.30am-7.15pm Ⓜ Můstek

Church of St Francis of Assisi (4, C3)

Run by a Czech order of cru-saders dating from the 12th century, the interior is circled

by alabaster saints and has a startling fresco of the *Last Judgement* by WL Reiner on its cupola. There are regular concerts featuring the second-oldest organ in Prague.
☎ box office 221 108 266
✉ Křížovnické náměstí Staré Město € church free, concerts 390/350Kč
☉ 10am-1pm & 2-6pm Tue-Sat, concerts at 9pm Apr-Oct Ⓜ Staroměstská

ALCHEMICAL KELLY

When Emperor Rudolf II made Prague the Imperial capital in 1583, the city experi-enced a 'Golden Age', in more ways than one. As well as his patronage of the arts and sciences, Rudolf was obsessed with alchemy, and was particularly pleased when the English magician Dr John Dee and his companion, the mystic and alchemist Edward Kelly, arrived on his doorstep. Kelly, who also claimed to have channelled an 'angelic' language called Enochian, began public demonstrations of his art, supposedly learnt from a mysterious tome and secret powders he had discovered in Wales. Rudolf was so impressed he knighted Kelly and installed him in the Powder Tower of Prague Castle to work on producing gold for the state. Unfortunately, Kelly's powers failed him and he was imprisoned in the White Tower in Golden Lane. He twice attempted to escape, breaking a leg each time, and died soon afterwards, taking his secrets with him.

Church of the Most Sacred Heart of Our Lord
(6, E4)

Erected in 1932 by Slovenian architect Josip Plečník, this unusual building looks like a stone freighter with a glass clock tower for a wheelhouse. It stands proudly in the middle of náměstí Jiřího z Poděbrad.

✉ náměstí Jiřího z Poděbrad 19, Vinohrady ⏱ services at 8am & 6pm Mon-Sat, 7am, 9am, 11am & 6pm Sun Ⓜ Jiřího z Poděbrad

Church of St Simon & St Juda
(4, D1-D2)

Both Mozart and Haydn played the organ at this ornate baroque church, squatting quietly in a peaceful corner of Josefov. Today it's under the care of the Prague Symphony Orchestra, which performs occasional concerts here; check the website for details.

☎ 222 321 068 🖥 www .kostel.cz ✉ cnr Dušní & U milosrydných, Josefov ⏱ open for services & occasional concerts Ⓜ Staroměstská

Klausen Synagogue
(4, C2-D2)

The present Klauzóva synagóga was built between 1689 and 1694, and underwent reconstruction in the 1880s. Today it holds the Jewish Museum's exhibition on Jewish customs, such as circumcision, bar and bat mitzvahs and kosher butchery. Upstairs is a mock-up of a 19th-century dining room.

☎ 222 317 191 🖥 www .jewishmuseum.cz ✉ U Starého hřbitova 3, Josefov € incl Jewish Museum 300/200Kč ⏱ 10am-4.30pm Sun-Fri Nov-Mar, 10am-6pm Sun-Fri Apr-Oct, closed Jewish holidays Ⓜ Staroměstská ♿ limited

Maisel Synagogue
(7, B1)

The neo-Gothic Maiselova synagóga was built in 1905 on the foundations of earlier temples that dated back to 1590. It's part of the Jewish Museum (p12), and hosts an exhibition on Jewish history in Bohemia from the 10th to the 18th centuries. More synagogue silver is on display.

☎ 222 317 191 🖥 www .jewishmuseum.cz ✉ Maiselova 10, Josefov € incl Jewish Museum 300/200Kč ⏱ 10am-4.30pm Sun-Fri Nov-Mar, 10am-6pm Sun-Fri Apr-Oct, closed Jewish holidays Ⓜ Staroměstská ♿ good

Pinkas Synagogue
(7, A1)

Part of the Jewish Museum (p12), Pinkasova Synagóga was built in 1535 and reconstructed in the 1950s as a memorial to the Bohemian and Moravian Jewish victims of the Nazis, with 77,297 names listed on its walls. Upstairs is a moving exhibition of drawings by children imprisoned in Terezín (p50).

☎ 222 317 191 🖥 www .jewishmuseum.cz ✉ Široká 3, Josefov € incl Jewish Museum 300/200Kč ⏱ 10am-4.30pm Sun-Fri Nov-Mar, 10am-6pm Sun-Fri Apr-Oct, closed Jewish holidays Ⓜ Staroměstská

Rotunda of the Holy Cross
(4, C5)

This 12th-century church (Kaple Sv Kříže) is also one

THE CZECHOSLOVAK HUSSITE CHURCH

Back in the early 1400s the priest and rector of Prague's Charles University, Jan Hus, began his campaign to reform what he saw as an increasingly corrupt Catholic church. They killed him, of course, but his reformist message had stirred many Czechs. Defenestrations, civil war and a Hussite King, George of Podebrady, followed. However, the Hussites were defeated at the Battle of the White Mountain in 1620 by the Catholic Habsburgs, and the Czech lands fell under Austrian rule for almost 300 years. After WWI a group of Catholic priests under the leadership of Karel Farský again urged reform. At Christmas 1919 they celebrated the whole church service in the Czech language for the first time, and on 11 January 1920 the independent Czechoslovak Hussite Church was proclaimed in St Nicholas Church on Old Town Square. Today there are more than 300 Hussite communities throughout the Czech Republic and Slovakia.

The simply stunning Spanish Synagogue

of the few Romanesque structures still standing in Prague and is one of the oldest buildings in the city. Its modest style comes as a relief after the soaring splendour of other local places of worship.
✉ cnr Konviktstá & Karoliny Světlé, Staré Město
🕐 services at 6pm Tue & 5pm Sun Ⓜ Národní Třída

Spanish Synagogue
(4, D2)
Dating from 1868 and part of the Jewish Museum (p12), this beautiful synagogue (Španělská synagóga) has a Moorish interior swirling with gilt, polychrome and arabesque motifs. There's an exhibition on 19th- and 20th-century Jewish history and a display of synagogue silver. Regular concerts are held here.
☎ 222 317 191 🖳 www .jewishmuseum.cz ✉ Věz-eňská 1, Josefov € incl Jewish Museum 300/200Kč
🕐 10am-4.30pm Sun-Fri Nov-Mar, 10am-6pm Sun-Fri

Apr-Oct, closed Jewish holidays Ⓜ Staroměstská
⅏ downstairs only

St Nicholas Church (7, C2)
Not to be confused with the church of the same name in Malostranské náměstí (p25), this elaborate baroque edifice was built by Kilian Dientzenhofer in 1735, and is adorned with vibrant frescoes and a huge crown-shaped chandelier donated by the Russian tsar, Nicholas II. It now belongs to the Czechoslovak Hussite Church (see opposite).
✉ Staroměstské náměstí, Staré Město 🕐 noon-4pm Mon, 10am-4pm Tue-Sat, noon-3pm Sun
Ⓜ Staroměstská

PARKS & GARDENS

Bílá Hora (6, A4)
The devastating 1620 Battle of the White Mountain took place in this now peaceful field on the western outskirts of Prague, routing Protestant

forces and ending Czech independence for three centuries. A footpath cuts through the corn to a little mound crowned with a memorial stone to the fallen.
✉ Řepská, access from Karlovarská, Břevnov € free
🕐 24hr Ⓜ Malostranská, then tram 22 or 25 to the end of the line ⅏ limited

Charles Square (6, C4)
Prague's biggest square (Karlovo náměstí) is in fact an inner-city park filled with birdsong, trees, flower beds, fountains and benches. The 'square' is sliced in two by the main road, Ječná. The northern half, watched over by the New Town Hall, is the busier, while the southern part has a small playground for children.
✉ Karlovo náměstí, Nové Město Ⓜ Karlovo Náměstí
⅏ excellent

Charles University Botanic Garden (6, C5)
Founded in 1775, and occupying this peaceful site since 1898, this is the

Czech Republic's oldest botanic garden, and one of Prague's most attractive green spaces. It has exotic trees, flower beds, water and herb gardens and a tropical glasshouse featuring cacti, papaya trees and a pond filled with catfish and giant lily pads.

✉ Viničná 7, Nové Město € grounds free, glasshouse 15Kč ⏱ 9am-6pm Mon-Fri Ⓜ Karlovo Náměstí ♿ good

Chotek Park (4, A1)

Landscaped in 1833, Chotkovy sady stretches east of the Summer Palace, and is Prague's oldest public park. Full of mature trees, but usually empty of people, the park allows splendid views south down the Vltava.

✉ Chotkovy sady, Hradčany Ⓜ Malostranská ♿ good

Franciscan Garden (4, E5)

The garden of the former Franciscan Ursuline convent (Františkánská zahrada) is now a neat, enclosed park, offering an oasis of greenery just a few steps away from the bustle of Wenceslas Square. Crowds of local office workers, shoppers and skateboarders vie with tourists for seating space on the benches, but it's still a pleasant place to catch your breath.

✉ Jungmannovo náměstí, Nové Město ⏱ 7am-10pm mid-Apr–mid-Sep, 7am-8pm mid-Sep–mid-Oct, 8am-7pm mid-Oct–mid-Apr Ⓜ Můstek ♿ good

Garden on the Ramparts (8, D3)

Apart from offering a spectacular vista over the rooftops of Malá Strana, the finely manicured Zahrada Na valech lets you get close to the castle's exterior, with its sloping concrete buffers. There are lots of seats where you can wind down, and occasional outdoor exhibitions.

☎ 224 373 368 🖥 www.hrad.cz ✉ Prague Castle, Hradčany ⏱ 10am-6pm Apr-Oct Ⓜ Malostranská, then tram 22 or 23 to Pražskýhrad ♿ good

Letná Gardens (6, C3)

Letenské sady has giddy views of the city and river from the concrete deck around its gigantic, creaking metronome. The device was built on the spot where an equally gigantic statue of Stalin was hoisted in 1955, then demolished in 1962. There are a few summer-time bars and communal seating areas where you can enjoy a beer or three under the trees.

✉ Letenské sady, Letná Ⓜ Malostranská, then tram No 12 to Čechův most; Hradčanská, then tram 1, 8, 25, 26, 51 or 56 to Sparta ♿ approach park from northern side

Palace Gardens Below Prague Castle (4, A2)

These lovely terraced formal gardens (Palácové Zahrady pod Pražským Hradem), on the southern slope of the castle, were created in the 17th and 18th centuries for the surrounding noble palaces. Laid out with statues, fountains and baroque summer houses, the gardens also host occasional music and drama performances.

☎ 257 010 401 🖥 www.palacovezahrady.cz ✉ Valdštejnské náměstí 3, Malá Strana € 69/39Kč ⏱ 10am-6pm Apr-Oct Ⓜ Malostranská ♿ limited

Royal Garden (5, B1)

Originally planted in 1535, Královská zahrada grants a royal respite from the crowded arena of Prague

Franciscan Garden is an oasis of greenery

Castle. Wander through groves of mature trees and past entrancing buildings, such as the Renaissance Ball-Game House and Summer Palace. If the fountain in front of the palace is flowing, you might get to hear why it's called the 'Singing Fountain'.

☎ 224 373 368 🖳 www .hrad.cz ✉ Mariánské hradby, Hradčany 🕑 10am-6pm Apr-Oct 🗐 Malostranská, then tram 22 or 23 to Pražskýhrad

Stromovka (6, C2)

The huge expanse of trees and clearings to the west of the Fairgrounds is often called Royal Deer Park because of its use as a hunting preserve in the Middle Ages. With its quiet lanes, duck ponds and weeping willows, it's a lovely place to escape crowds.

✉ Stromovka, Bubeneč 🗐 Nádraží Holešovice, then tram 5, 12, 17, 53 or 54 to Výstaviště 🕭 good

A virtual riot of autumn colour at the Palace Gardens

Vojan Park (4, A3)

Once part of a Carmelite convent, this sleepy park (Vojanovy sady) is Prague's oldest, and was established in 1248, though it only opened to the public in 1955. It's a peaceful spot, with a small children's play area near the front entrance.

✉ U lužického semináře, Malá Strana 🕑 8am-7pm, to 5pm Nov-Mar 🗐 Malostranská 🕭 good

Wallenstein Garden (4, A2)

This magnificent 17th-century formal garden (Valdštejnská zahrada) is dominated by a grand loggia,

painted with scenes from the Trojan War. Nearby, mysterious stony monsters lurk between the cracks of an artificial grotto. There's also a duck pond and an aviary. The statues around the park are copies; the originals were stolen by the Swedes during the Thirty Years' War.

✉ Letenská, Malá Strana 🕑 9am-6pm May-Sep, 10am-6pm Apr & Oct 🗐 Malostranská 🕭 good

SQUARES & STREETS

Celetná Ulice (7, D2)

The name of this pedestrianised strip of pastel façades,

linking Old Town Square with náměstí Republiky, derives from the word *caltnéři,* which referred to the street's 14th-century bakers of *calty* (buns).It's occupied by a string of jewellery and crystal shops these days.

✉ Celetná ulice, Staré Město 🗐 Náměstí Republiky 🕭 excellent

Hradčanské Náměstí (5, A3)

Prague Castle's 'front yard' is an attraction in its own right: a large paved space bordered by the architectural melange of the Archbishop's Palace and the loud *sgraffito* (multilayered murals) of the Schwarzenberg Palace. The

square's small park is punctured by Ferdinand Brokoff's plague column, marking the Black Death's death in 1679.
✉ Hradčanské náměstí, Hradčany Ⓜ Malostranská ♿ excellent

Jan Palach Square (7, A1)
This modest concrete and grass patchwork (náměsti Jana Palacha) is dedicated to philosophy student Jan Palach, who set himself ablaze on 16 January 1969 in protest against the Warsaw Pact invasion of Prague. A death mask plaque of Palach is attached to the Univerzity Karlovy faculty he attended across the road.
✉ náměstí Jana Palacha, Josefov Ⓜ Staroměstská ♿ excellent

Lucerna Passage
(4, E6-F6)
This extensive, somewhat gloomy, Art Nouveau labyrinth (Pasáž Lucerna) under Lucerna Palace is bordered by Wenceslas Square, Štěpánská, Vjámě and Vodičkova. There

are many shops, restaurants and a music club, as well as an upside-down copy of the famous St Wenceslas statue, by artist David Černý, dangling outside Lucerna cinema.
✉ Lucerna Passage, Nové Město Ⓜ Můstek ♿ good

Malé Náměstí (7, C3)
'Little Square' is surrounded by neo-Renaissance and baroque façades, including the *sgraffito*-decorated VJ Rott building, and has a wrought-iron fountain at its centre. Unfortunately it's often choked with pedestrian traffic moving between Old Town Square and Charles Bridge.
✉ Malé náměstí, Staré Město Ⓜ Staroměstská ♿ good

Malostranské Náměstí
(5, C3)
Much of Malá Strana's busiest square is taken up by a car park and the enormous perimeter of the baroque St Nicholas Church (p25), with

the brooding Liechtenstein Palace taking plenty of space too. There are some good bars, pubs and restaurants around the square.
✉ Malostranské náměstí, Malá Strana Ⓜ Malostranská ♿ good

Maltézské Náměstí
(5, C4)
Duck down quiet Prokopská to this attractive square, named after the Knights of Malta, who established a monastery nearby. Beyond the statue of St John the Baptist is a side-street glimpse of the Church of Our Lady Below the Chain.
✉ Maltézské náměstí, Malá Strana Ⓜ Malostranská ♿ good

Na Příkopě (7, E4)
Prague's part pedestrianised high street, lined with fashion outlets, restaurants and shopping arcades, slants down from náměstí Republiky to the northern tip of Wenceslas Square. Chain-stores and shopping

SIGNS OF THE TIMES
One distinctive feature of many Prague streets is the array of colourful house signs gracing the fronts of older buildings. House numbering only began in 1770, so before then, residents created symbols that related to their trade or some event associated with that building. Nerudova (opposite) in Malá Strana has a particularly rich supply. The magnificently crafted work of art – shown right – for the House of the Three Fiddles (No 12), for example, belonged to a violin-maker whose customers included Beethoven; while the House of the Two Suns (No 47) was originally home to a goldsmith. There are many more such signs throughout the Old Town, including the Golden Snake (Karlova 18) and the Blue Star (Old Town Square 25).

GOLDEN LANE

Golden Lane (8, E1-F1) is the narrow and usually sardine-packed little thoroughfare in the northeastern corner of Prague Castle. It came into existence some time after 1484, when the erection of a new outer castle wall created a passageway between itself and the older Romanesque fortifications. Originally called Zlatnická ulička (Goldsmith's Lane) after resident goldsmith guild members, it was a mini shanty town of tiny dwellings that were later occupied by castle artillerymen. Today it's essentially a tourist-trap shopping mall (and one you have to pay to get into), with a row of 11 houses operating as souvenir shops, selling everything from jewellery to reproduction armour. There are often queues to get into some of these minute shops, so claustrophobics beware! There's also a café and a crossbow range. At one end is the White Tower, where the alchemist Edward Kelly was held (see p33), while at the other is the Daliborka Tower, one-time gaol of the 15th-century knight Dalibor, whose fiddle-playing inspired Smetana's eponymous opera.

malls dominate the scene, while modern art installations appear in summer.

✉ Na příkopě, Nové Město Ⓜ Můstek, Náměstí Republiky ♿ excellent

Nerudova (5, B3)

The steep final steep stretch of the Royal Way was named after the writer Jan Neruda, who once lived at No 47. It's famous for its elegant baroque façades and colourful house signs, including the House of the Three Fiddles (No 12), the House of the Golden Horseshoe (No 34) and the House of the Green Lobster (No 43).

✉ Nerudova, Malá Strana Ⓜ Malostranská ♿ limited

Pařížská Třída (7, C1)

Outdoor cafés and upmarket shops mingle with stately Art Nouveau apartment buildings on tree-lined 'Parisian Avenue', which swishes from Old Town Square north to the Vltava.

✉ Pařížská třída, Josefov Ⓜ Staroměstská ♿ excellent

Wenceslas Square (4, E5)

Prague's biggest square, Václavské náměstí is an elongated boulevard lined with shops and restaurants and dominated at its southern end by the National Museum (p16). It was the scene of protests against the Soviet invasion in 1968 and 1969, and of celebrations in 1989 when the communist regime collapsed. In summer it becomes an outdoor art gallery for avant-garde sculptures.

✉ Václavské náměstí, Nové Město Ⓜ Můstek, Muzeum ♿ good

Golden Lane – it doesn't look like a tourist trap

JEWISH TOWN

Jews had been living in Prague for 300 years before the church authorities decreed, in the 13th century, that they should move into a walled ghetto and live apart from their Christian neighbours. The Jewish population was subject to intermittent repression and pogroms over the succeeding centuries. The enlightened Emperor Joseph II brought in antidiscriminatory laws in the 1780s, but it wasn't until 1848 that the ghetto walls were pulled down. The Jewish district was renamed Josefov in his honour. This quarter, which had become seriously run-down, was largely cleared between 1893 and 1910, and was divided in two by the Art Nouveau Pařížská Třída (p39). The community was almost wiped out by the Nazis, and many Jews emigrated after the war. Today only about 6000 Jews remain in Prague.

QUIRKY PRAGUE

John Lennon Wall (4, A4)
From Lennon's 1980 murder until the communists' 1989 downfall, this was where activists defied the antipop authorities by scribbling Beatles lyrics and peace slogans. Lennonova zed got whitewashed in 1998 but today it's once again a psychedelic mess of spray-painted pictures and names, now scrawled by tourists, in numerous languages.
⊠ Velkopřevorské náměstí, Malá Strana Ⓜ Malostranská
& good

Museum of the Infant Jesus of Prague (5, C4)
The Church of Our Lady Victorious is dedicated to the cult of the Infant Jesus, which began in 1628, when Polyxena, a Spanish noble-woman, presented a wax statue of the Child Jesus to the friars here. The Muzeum Pražského Jezulátka upstairs displays its wardrobe of embroidered cloaks, while the figure itself sits in the big marble altar on the right side of the church.
☎ 257 533 646 🖳 www
.karmel.at/prag-jesu

⊠ Karmelitská 9, Malá Strana Ⓔ free ⊙ 9.30am-5.30pm Mon-Sat
Ⓜ Malostranská

Muzeum Miniatur (2, A2)
Anatoly Koněnko is a Siberian artist who produces the tiniest works possible. All the pieces are just about visible in this extraordinary museum. His works include a painted train on a human hair, a pair of gold horseshoes for a flea, a 3.2mm-high replica of the Eiffel Tower and the world's most minuscule book.
☎ 233 352 371 ⊠ Stra-hovské nádvoří 10, Strahov
Ⓔ 50/30Kč ⊙ 10am-5pm
Ⓜ Malostranská, then tram 22 or 23 to Pohořelec

In the words of the famous Beatle – give peace a chance

PRAGUE FOR CHILDREN

Prague is a city that has everything families could wish for. Choose from adventurous playgrounds, lively puppet shows, street theatre, child-friendly museums, and, of course, lots of cash-hungry stores filled to the brim with tempting stuff to cart home. Czechs are usually family-oriented and most hotels have a discounted price for children. Unlike many European countries, you won't see many children out with their parents at night, or in restaurants, although a growing number of eateries do offer child menus. Nearly all tourist attractions have reduced child tariffs.

Dětský ostrov (4, A6-B6)
Prague's smallest island (Children's Island) offers a leafy respite from the busy city streets, with a few swings, climbing frames and a sandpit to occupy toddlers, as well as a mini football pitch and netball court for older siblings. There are plenty of benches for the less energetic, and there's also a restaurant (p80) on the island.
✉ Dětský ostrov Ⓜ Anděl
♿ good

Divadlo Spejbla a Hurvínka (6, B3)
A famous theatre established in 1930 by Josef Skupa and named after his father-and-son marionette creations (Spejbl and Hurvínek, respectively), which have since figured prominently in many Czech childhoods. The puppet shows range from straight comedy or drama to material with a visually 'grotesque' bent that has adult appeal.
☎ 224 316 784 ✉ Dejvická 38, Dejvice € 50Kč ⏰ box office 10am-2pm & 3-6pm Tue-Fri 1-5pm, Sat & Sun; performances 10am Tue-Fri, 2pm & 4.30pm Sat & Sun Ⓜ Dejvická

Fairgrounds (6, C2)
The Fairgrounds (Výstaviště) is a sprawling enclave of pavilions, theatres and amusement rides (particularly

KID CARE

The turnover of babysitting agencies in Prague is often as high as the turnover of their charges, but a few worth contacting are **Babysitting Praha** (☎ 602 885 074) with 24-hour care on weekends, charging from 80Kč per hour; **Tetty** (☎ 233 340 766; www.tetty.cz); and **Babysitting – Markéta Tomková** (☎ 608 082 868; tomkovam@seznam.cz), which has English and French speakers at hand.

when one of Prague's major fairs is on). Theatre and concerts are held in the Spiral Theatre (p91) and Goja Music Hall (p90), while kids might enjoy the spectacle of the computer-conducted Křižík Fountain 'dancing' to music.
🖥 www.krizikovafontana.cz ✉ U Výstaviště, Holešovice € amusement rides 20-40Kč Ⓜ Nádraží Holešovice, then tram 5, 12, 17, 53 or 54 to Výstaviště ♿ good

Laser Game Fun Centre (4, D5)
Subterranean video-game arcade in the Palác Metro mall, with the usual racing, kickboxing and shoot-'em-

Puppet on a string

up diversions. There's also a 'laser-quest' game arena for more active fun, and an Internet café (1Kč per minute).
☎ 224 221 188 ✉ Národni třída 25, Nové Město € laser game 149Kč, credit chips 10Kč (most games 1 credit) ⏰ 10am-midnight Ⓜ Národní Třída

Maze (5, A5)
This mirror maze (Bludiště), atop Petřín Hill, is where kids get to distort themselves with no lasting consequences. There's also a diorama called 'Battle against the Swedes on Charles Bridge in 1648', set at the end of the Thirty Years' War.
✉ Petřínské sady, Malá Strana € 50/40Kč ⏰ 10am-10pm May-Aug, 10am-7pm Apr & Sep, 10am-6pm Oct, 10am-5pm Sat & Sun Nov-Mar Ⓜ Národní Třída, then tram 22, 23 or 57 to Újezd, then funicular railway

Museum of Marionette Culture (7, A3)
Rooms filled with a multitude of authentic, colourfully dressed marionettes from the late 17th to early 19th centuries. Star attractions are the Czech figures Spejbl and Hurvínek (see p41). The museum is upstairs inside the courtyard.
☎ 222 220 928 🖥 www.puppetart.com ✉ Karlova 12, Staré Město € 100Kč ⏰ 10am-8pm Ⓜ Staroměstská

National Technical Museum (6, C3-D3)
One of the biggest technical museums in the world, with steam trains, planes, vintage

cars and motorbikes on show, as well as exhibitions on astronomy, photography and acoustics, a working TV studio and a mock-up of a coalmine.
☎ 220 399 111 🖥 www.ntm.cz ✉ Kostelní 42, Holešovice € 70/30Kč, audio guide 50Kč, free from noon 1st Fri of month ⏰ 9am-5pm Tue-Fri, 10am-6pm Sat & Sun Ⓜ Hradčanská, then tram 1, 8, 25, 26, 51 or 56 to Letenské náměstí

Prague Zoo (6, B1)
You could spend the whole day at this enormous park, where residents include gorillas, elephants, lions, tigers, penguins and the endangered Przewalski's horse, the zoo's symbol. Recent additions include the 'Indonesian Jungle' (a glass-domed mini ecosystem) and the 'Children's Zoo', featuring farm animals, a paddling pool and a toy train.
☎ 296 112 111 🖥 www.zoopraha.cz ✉ U Trojského zámku 3, Troja € 90/60Kč Apr-Sep, 70/40Kč Oct-Mar ⏰ 9am-5pm Mar, 9am-6pm Apr-May & Sep-Oct, 9am-7pm Jun-Aug, 9am-4pm Nov-Feb Ⓜ Nádraží Holešovice, then bus 112 to Zoo Praha ♿ good, but some enclosures are inaccessible

Public Transport Museum (6, A3-B3)
There's a truck load of trams and buses in this old depot, the oldest being a horse-drawn tramcar from 1886, while other passenger vehicles and freight cars span most of the 20th century. A free guidebook tells you all

A maze of mirrors on the wall...

you need to know, and if that whets your appetite, jump on Nostalgic Tram 91 for a rattle round town (p52).

☎ 296 124 905
✉ Patočkova 4, Střešovičky
€ 25/10Kč ⌚ 9am-5pm Sat & Sun & public holidays late Mar–mid-Nov
Ⓜ Hradčanská, then tram No 1, 8, 18, 56 or 57 to Vozovna Střešovice ♿ good

Sea World (6, D2)
Over 300 species of fish and other sea creatures are on show at Mořský Svět, a modern aquarium at the Fairgrounds. Reef sharks, clown fish, starfish and beautiful sea anemones compete for attention downstairs, while on the upper level there's a collection of soft and hard corals.

☎ 220 103 275 💻 www .morsky-svet.cz ✉ Fairgrounds, Holešovice

€ 120/70Kč ⌚ 10am-7pm
Ⓜ Nádraží Holešovice, then tram 5, 12, 17, 53 or 54 to U Výstaviště ♿ ground floor only

Štefánik Observatory (5, A6)
Sitting prettily in the rose garden atop Petřín Hill, this observatory's telescope offers you a chance to view the stars at night, surrounding buildings during the day, or the sun (projected onto a screen) on cloudless days. There's a small exhibition on protons and electrons, and displays of vintage instruments.

☎ 257 320 540 💻 www .observatory.cz ✉ Petřínské sady, Malá Strana € 30/20Kč
⌚ 7-9pm Tue-Fri, 10am-noon & 2-9pm Mar, 2-7pm & 9-11pm Tue-Fri, 10am-noon, 2-6pm & 7-11pm Sat & Sun Apr-Aug, 2-6pm &

8-10pm Tue-Fri, 10am-noon, 2-7pm & 9-11pm Sat & Sun Sep, 7-9pm Tue-Fri, 10am-noon, 2-6pm & 7-9pm Oct, 6-8pm Tue-Fri, 10am-noon & 2-8pm Sat & Sun Nov-Feb
Ⓜ Národní Třída, then tram 22, 23 or 57 to Újezd, then funicular railway

Toy Museum (8, F1)
A sizable collection of vintage toys, from 19th-century wooden dolls and tin train sets to plastic robots from the 1960s. The top floor is dominated by Barbie, in all her costumes, accompanied by a clutch of Ken dolls and other friends. There are several flights of stairs to climb before you reach the exhibition.

☎ 224 372 294 ✉ Jiřská 6, Prague Castle, Hradčany
€ 60/30Kč ⌚ 9.30am-5.30pm Ⓜ Malostranská, Hradčanská

Trips & Tours

WALKING TOURS
Josefov

Josefov (Jewish Town) was once a bustling Jewish ghetto dating back to the 13th century, until it was reconstructed and gentrified in the late 19th century. Start at **Franz Kafka's birthplace** (**1**), and head north along

Jan Palach's death mask memorial

Maiselova past the **Maisel Synagogue** (**2**; p34) to the **Renaissance High Synagogue** (**3**); across the laneway is Prague's oldest and most important Jewish temple, the **Old-New Synagogue** (**4**; p13). Go west down U starého hřbitova alongside the **Old Jewish Cemetery** (**5**), Europe's oldest. Pass the **Klausen Synagogue** (**6**; p34) and **Ceremonial Hall** (**7**; p26), before heading north to Břehová. Turn left, then left again onto 17.listopadu for the **Museum of Decorative Arts** (**8**; p20). Cross the road to **Jan Palach Square** (**9**; p38), and gaze up at the massive **Rudolfinum** (**10**). Re-cross 17.listopadu and go east along Široká to **Pinkas Synagogue** (**11**; p34), a memorial to Jews who died during WWII. Continue east until you get to the magnificent Moorish **Spanish Synagogue** (**12**; p35); outside stands a surreal statue of

Kafka. Continue east and at Haštalské náměstí drop by **Chez Marcel** (**13**; p68) for a quick bite before turning north up Anežská to see medieval art at the **Convent of St Agnes** (**14**; p28).

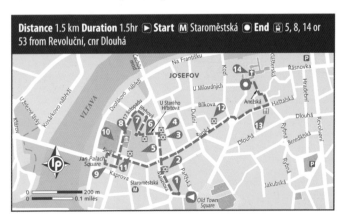

Distance 1.5 km **Duration** 1.5hr ▶ **Start** Ⓜ Staroměstská ◉ **End** 🚊 5, 8, 14 or 53 from Revoluční, cnr Dlouhá

Royal Way

The ancient coronation route starts from náměstí Republiky. First gaze at the Art Nouveau splendour of the **Municipal House** (**1**; p15), then stroll under the **Powder Tower** (**2**; p32) and then down **Celetná Ulice** (**3**; p37). Admire the cubist **House of the Black Madonna** (**4**), and do coffee at Grand Café Orient (p76) upstairs, before doubling back up Celetná and swinging north up Králodvorská, past the **Hotel Paříž** (**5**; p98) to Kotva. Turn left into Jakubská and walk down to **St James Church** (**6**), then cross Malá Štupartská and amble through Týn Court. Exit at the western end and go past the northern door of **Týn Church** (**7**; p22) into Old Town Square. Veer southwest to emerge into pastel-lined **Malé Náměstí** (**8**; p38). Bear left, then right into Karlova. Follow Karlova through the tourist crush and along the hulking **Klementinum** (**9**; p31) to Křižovnicka and cross over **Charles Bridge** (**10**; p11). Head up Mostecká

Standing room only on Charles Bridge

into the bustle of **Malostranské náměstí** (**11**; p38), to be greeted by the baroque **St Nicholas Church** (**12**; p25). Cross to the square's northern side and turn left into **Nerudova** (**13**; p39), the steep road that eases you past beer halls and tearooms to **Prague Castle** (**14**; p8).

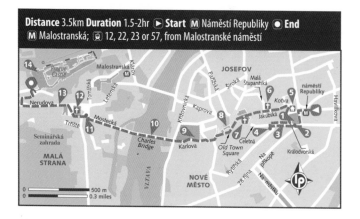

Distance 3.5km **Duration** 1.5–2hr ▶ **Start** Ⓜ Náměstí Republiky ● **End**
Ⓜ Malostranská; 🚋 12, 22, 23 or 57, from Malostranské náměstí

Upriver to Vyšehrad

To follow the Vltava towards the ancient citadel, Vyšehrad, begin opposite the **National Theatre** (**1**; p92), which has magnificent views and down river. Head south down Masarykovo nábřeží and walk onto Slovanský ostrov, calling in at **Mánes Gallery** (**2**; p29) to see the latest contemporary art. Back on the 'mainland', cross the road; **Don Pedro** (**3**; p72) makes a good lunch stop. A little further along, the fantastical **Dancing Building** (**4**; p30) is Prague's most striking modern architecture. Continue south, on Rašínovo nábřeží, and you'll come to Palackého náměstí, lorded over by the **František Palacký Monument** (**5**; p31), a grand tribute to the 19th-century historian and writer. Continuing south, cross the road to the river side once more to truly appreciate some of the most vibrant Art Nouveau façades in the city, with swirling organic motifs and colourful mosaics. At the corner with Svobodova is the old **Podskalí Customs House** (**6**; p27), a 16th-century building that's now a small museum and pub – perfect for a cold beer. Passing under the railway bridge you'll see the cubist **Villa Libušina** (**7**). Continue walking to the long flight of steps up to **Vyšehrad** (**8**; p23), for amazing panoramic views of the river.

Distance 2km **Duration** 1hr ▶ **start**
🚊 17, 21 or 22 ● **End** 🚊 16, 17 or 21

Theatrical reflections on the Vltava River

North to Stromovka

This walk crosses the river and goes into Prague's biggest park. From the metro station, walk north up 17.listopadu, to the **Museum of Decorative Arts** (**1**; p20) on the right and the magnificent **Rudolfinum** (**2**) on the left. Enjoy the view of Prague Castle from Jan Palach Square. Continue along this road till you get to the river. Cross Čechův most, climb the stairs to **Letná Gardens** (**3**; p36), catch your breath and enjoy a panoramic view of the city. Make your way east, stopping at **Brasserie Ullman** (**4**; pp79–80) for lunch, or the informal beer garden. Leave the park at Kostelní and walk east until you come to the junction with Dukelských hrdinů. Take this street north. Don't miss the excellent, extensive displays at the **Centre for Modern & Contemporary Art** (**5**; p14) here. Continue north, passing under the railway bridge and emerging in front of the **Fairgrounds** (**6**; pp41–2). Peek at the sculptures at the **Lapidárium** (**7**; p26) and the fishy inhabitants of **Sea World** (**8**; p43). Kids love the amusements and rides behind the Palace of Industry. From here, it's a pleasant amble westwards into the vast bosky **Stromovka** (**9**; p37) to relax under weeping willows away from crowds.

The simply breathtaking Rudolfinum

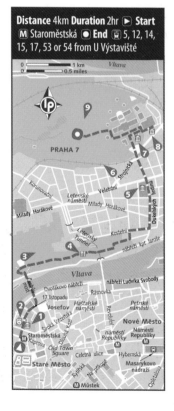

Distance 4km **Duration** 2hr ▶ **Start** Ⓜ Staroměstská ⊙ **End** 🚃 5, 12, 14, 15, 17, 53 or 54 from U Výstaviště

DAY TRIPS
Karlštejn
(1, A3)

Karlštejn Castle's foundations were laid in 1348 by Emperor Charles IV, who used the crag-top edifice as a safe repository for the Imperial Crown Jewels and his collection of holy relics. The castle's reputation for impregnability led Emperor Sigismund to deposit both the Bohemian and Imperial treasures here at the outbreak of the Hussite revolt, and the place was later used as a public records office. The castle was given a fresh medieval shape in the 1890s, and is now stormed by foreign armies of tourists most days; it's the most popular and best-preserved castle in the Czech Republic. Standard tours visit internal features such as the **Knights' Hall**, bedecked with coats of arms, the **Hall of Ancestors**, filled with 17th-century royal portraits, and the **Treasury**, where you can see replicas of the glittering crown jewels, but it's the view of the surrounding countryside that's most impressive.

If time permits, take a peep at the curious **Muzeum Betlémů**, down in the village, with its collection of intricate Nativity scenes. The huge, mechanical 'Royal Crib of Karlštejn', with its 40 moving puppets, will make you come over all Christmassy.

INFORMATION
25km southwest of Prague

- Ⓜ Hlavní Nádraží, then local train (50min; 58Kč return) to Karlštejn, then a 20-25min walk to the castle through town or 10min horse and cart ride (150Kč per person). Note: some returning trains only go as far as Smíchovské Nádraží
- ☎ 311 681 617
- 🖥 www.hradkarlstejn.cz
- € 50min tour Rte 1 200/100Kč, Rte 2 (Chapel of the Holy Cross) 300/100Kč; Rte 2 Jul-Nov only, by reservation; museum 40Kč
- ⏱ 9am-noon & 1-3pm Tue-Sun Mar & Nov-Dec, 9am-noon & 1-4pm Tue-Sun Apr & Oct, 9am-noon & 12.30-5pm May-Jun & Sep, 9am-noon & 12.30-6pm Tue-Sun Jul & Aug, 9am-noon & 1-3pm 1st week in Jan, closed Feb & day after public holidays; museum 9am-7pm Jul-Sep
- ⓘ ticket office in main courtyard

Kutná Hora (1, C2)

The discovery of silver ore in the 13th century quickly made Kutná Hora Bohemia's most important town; it became home to the royal mint in 1308, and later the royal residence. Everything changed when the silver ran out in the 16th century, and Kutná Hora's decline was hastened by the Thirty Years' War. Now an attractive and very popular tourist destination, its churches and historic architecture contributed to it being World Heritage listed by Unesco in 1996.

At the heart of town is a pretty central square, Palackého náměstí. To the southwest the **Czech Museum of Silver** (České Muzeum Stříbra), houses exhibitions on the industry, as well as an original mine shaft which you can explore on guided tours. Further along in this direction are the magnificent Gothic spires of **St Barbara's Church** (Chrám sv Barbory), begun in 1380 but only finished in the late 19th century. Don't miss the unique 15th-century murals depicting silver miners and minters at work.

Northeast of the centre, in the suburb of Sedlec, is the grimly fascinating ossuary in the **Chapel of All Saints**. The chapel became a skeletal repository in the 14th century, after plague overburdened the adjacent cemetery. In 1870 a woodcarver named František Rint set about arranging the myriad bones into their current patterns, which include crosses, chalices, a coat of arms, and a chandelier made of every bone in the human body.

INFORMATION
70km southeast of Prague

- 🚊 Kutná Hora (1-1½hr, 112Kč return), then Tourist Bus (May-Sep, 15min, 15Kč one way) to ossuary or St Barbara's Church, or local train (8min, 10Kč one way) to Kutná Hora město station, then 10-15min walk (for many return services to Prague, change at Kolín; some trains terminate at Masarykovo nádraží station)
- ☎ 0327 512 378
- 🖳 www.kutnohorsko.cz
- € Czech Museum of Silver 60/30Kč, mine tour 110/70Kč; St Barbara's Church 30/15Kč; ossuary 35/20Kč
- 🕑 Czech Museum of Silver 9am-5pm Tue-Sun Apr & Oct, 9am-6pm Tue-Sun May, Jun & Sep, 10am-6pm Tue-Sun Jul & Aug, closed Nov-Mar; St Barbara's Church 9am-6pm Tue-Sun May-Sep, 9am-noon & 1-4.30pm Tue-Sun Apr & Oct, 10am-noon & 1-4pm Tue-Sun Nov-Mar; ossuary 8am-6pm Apr-Sep, 9am-noon & 1-5pm Oct, 9am-noon &1-4pm Nov-Mar
- ℹ️ information centre, (Palackého náměstí 377); open 9am-6.30pm Mon-Fri, 9am-5pm Sat & Sun Apr-Oct, 9am-5pm Mon-Fri Nov-Mar

Terezín (1, A1)

The massive citadel of Terezín, with 4km of walls and moats, was built in 1780 by Emperor Joseph II as defence against Prussian aggression, and was subsequently used as a garrison post and then a prisoner-of-war camp during WWI. In 1940 the **Lesser Fortress** became a Gestapo prison, and by late 1941 the Main Fortress had been turned into a Nazi transit camp that saw the passage of over 150,000 Jews en route to extermination camps. Sadly, visiting international observers were fooled into believing that Terezín was a happy, self-governing Jewish 'refuge', with shops, schools, theatre and even a jazz band. At its peak, Terezín held 60,000 people in a space originally meant for 5000; 35,000 Jews imprisoned here died from disease, starvation or suicide.

INFORMATION

50km northwest of Prague

- Ⓜ Florenc, then bus from Florenc bus station (73Kč)
- ☎ 0416 782 576
- 🖥 www.pamatnik-terezin.cz
- € ticket to museum, crematorium & Lesser Fortress 180/140Kč; individual sites 160/130Kč
- 🕙 Museum of the Ghetto & Magdeburg Barracks 9am-6pm Apr-Oct, 9am-5.30pm Nov-Mar; crematorium 10am-5pm Sun-Fri Apr-Oct, 10am-4pm Sun-Fri Nov-Mar; Lesser Fortress 8am-6pm Apr-Oct, 8am-4.30pm Nov-Mar
- ⓘ ticket offices in Museum of the Ghetto and Lesser Fortress

Inside the monumental Main Fortress, on Komenského, is the **Museum of the Ghetto**, which documents the way Jewish people tried to conduct their lives in Terezín via videos, photographs, personal letters and artwork; drawings by some of the many incarcerated children are also on display at the Pinkas Synagogue (p34) in Prague. At the corner of Tyršova and Vodárenská, the former **Magdeburg Barracks** holds an exhibition on the talented musicians, artists and writers who passed through Terezín before being murdered elsewhere, while 100m south of the fortress walls is the **Crematorium**, located in the Jewish cemetery. The Lesser Fortress is a challenging place to visit with its chilling barracks, cells and morgues. You can see it via a self-guided tour.

Mělník (1, B1)

The charming little town of Mělník, 30km north of Prague, is Bohemia's modest wine-growing region centre. The former Hussite stronghold was destroyed by the Swedes during the Thirty Years' War, but was soon rebuilt, and retains a strong historical identity. It's the walled Old Town, with its attractive square and friendly, well-stocked wine bars, that's the point of interest for day-tripping tourists; beyond lies the unremarkable sprawl of the modern town.

INFORMATION
30km north of Prague
- Ⓜ Nádraží Holešovice, then bus (1hr, 38Kč)
- ☎ 0206 62 75 03 9am-5pm May-Sep
- 🕙 chateau 10am-6pm; ossuary 9.30am-12.30pm & 1.15-4pm Tue-Sun
- € chateau 70/50Kč; ossuary 50/30Kč
- ⓘ information centre, (náměstí Míru 11); open 9am-5pm Mon-Fri Oct-Apr

The dominating Renaissance **Mělník Chateau** has been in the possession of the Lobkowicz family since the 18th century, apart from a 40-year interlude when it was confiscated by the communist regime. It's been open to the public since 1992, though it's still undergoing restoration. You can wander through the former living quarters, including a bedroom, a study and dining rooms, furnished with period antiques and family mementos, as well as the 14th-century chapel and staircases decorated with hunting trophies. Afterwards, you can buy wines from the Lobkowicz estate in the castle shop.

Next to the chateau is the 15th-century Gothic **Church of Sts Peter and Paul**, with its commanding baroque tower. The old crypt is now an **ossuary**, packed with bones of some 10,000 people (disinterred to make room for 16th-century plague victims), arranged in patterns. Skulls deemed to be of Germanic origin were placed down face-first. Look out for the vintage graffito reading, in Latin, 'Slaup from Žlutice was here, 1535'.

ORGANISED TOURS

If you've had enough of organising yourself, let someone else do it for you. There are numerous companies in Prague offering guided bus and walking tours of the city, if you want to play 'follow the umbrella', though there's usually little difference between them. There are also more imaginative operators running excursions to the country or novel ways to get acquainted with Prague.

City Walks

Runs several tours, including the Ghost Trail, Franz Kafka Walk and Legends & Mystery Tour, revealing Prague's esoteric side. Its six-hour Ultimate Tour, by tram, boat and on foot, gives a comprehensive overview of the city.
☎ 608 200 912 ✉ meet under Astronomical Clock, Staré Město € from 300/250Kč 1½ or 2hr walk; 6hr Ultimate Tour 1000Kč; ☼ vary

Fun in Prague

Offers a wide choice of tours and activities, ranging from touristy tramps through the Old Town and boat trips to rafting, horse-riding and paintballing excursions.
☎ 724 371 392 🖳 www .funinprague.com ✉ meet at Křižovnické náměstí, Staré Město € walks 300-350Kč, sports 1000-2000Kč ☼ vary

Menhir Travellers Club

Explore some of the secret corners of the Bohemian countryside, taking in ruined castles and monasteries, prehistoric monuments and other things most tourists never get to see. The full-day trips include lunch.
☎ 732 905 381 7-10am & 9-11pm, 732 927 606 1-5pm 🖳 www.menhirclub.cz ✉ meet under statue of St Wenceslas, Wenceslas Square € 1350Kč ☼ departs at 9am Fri & Sat Apr-Oct

Nostalgic Tram No 91
(6, A3)

There are several tramcars, made between 1908 and 1942, navigating Nostalgic Tramline No 91, a special sightseeing run. Trams depart from the Střešovice depot beside the Public Transport Museum (p42) and wind their way past Prague Castle, through Malá Strana, across Wenceslas Square and up to the Fairgrounds and back.
☎ 233 343 349 ✉ Patočkova 4, Střešovice € 25/10Kč ☼ on the hour noon-6pm Sat, Sun & public holidays Apr–mid-Nov

Prague Venice (4, 3)

Hop aboard a vintage canal boat for a 30-minute cruise taking in the hidden arches of Charles Bridge, the Čertovka canal and other riverside sights. The price includes a drink and ice cream.
☎ 603 819 947 🖳 www .prague-venice.cz ✉ Karlův Most, Staré Město € 270/135Kč ☼ 10.30am-8pm Apr-Jun & Sep, 10.30am-10.30pm Jul & Aug, 10.30am-7pm Oct-Dec, 10.30am-6pm Jan-Mar

Praha Bike (3, C8)

Jump on a bike for a guided cycle through the city, or an easy peddle through the parks. Trips outside Prague can also be arranged, and helmets, locks and maps are provided. Bikes are available for private rental too.
☎ 732 388 880 🖳 www.pra habike.cz ✉ Dlouhá 24, Staré Město € 2½hr guided ride 440Kč ☼ tours at 11.30am, 2.30pm & 5.30pm Mar-Oct

Wittmann Tours (3, A1)

Jewish guide service offering bus and walking tours of sights of Jewish interest in and around Prague. Trips further afield include the concentration camps of Auschwitz and Mauthausen, and individually designed tours can also be arranged.
☎ 222 252 472 🖳 www .wittmann-tours.com ✉ Mánesova 8, Nové Město r2hr walking tour from 500Kč, private tours from €45 per hr

Touring the Staré Město on a rented mountain bike

Shopping

As in most other big European capitals, you can now buy pretty much anything you can think of in Prague, and new shops are opening all the time to tempt the increasing numbers of foreign tourists in search of something special, and to meet the demands of the increasingly affluent and cosmopolitan residents. Beautiful standards such as Bohemian crystal, Czech garnets and traditional ceramics remain popular, while home-grown fashions, music, wines and homewares are also proving a success. With the array of often excellent, and reasonably priced, locally produced goods swelling all the time, you'll probably find yourself sorely tempted to loosen the purse strings at every turn.

Ready, set, shop

Shopping Areas

The city centre's single biggest – and the most exhausting – retail zone is **Wenceslas Square** (4, E5-F5), permanently crowded with browsing visitors and locals dashing in and out of their favourite stores. Fashion boutiques, music megastores, department stores and gigantic book emporia are all to be found here. Many intriguing outlets are hidden in side alleys such as **Lucerna Passage** (4, E6-F6).

The other main shopping drag is the extended thoroughfare comprising **Národní třída** (4, C5), **28.října** (4, E4) and **Na příkopě** (7, E4). Most of the big shops are concentrated along Na příkopě, which is studded with malls and a variety of upmarket stores. Elsewhere, **Pařížská** (7, C1) is the place to go for international designer chic, while the winding streets between the Old Town Square and Charles Bridge are regularly thronged with tourists perusing the puppets, 'cheeky' T-shirts and Russian dolls, which spill out from numerous junky souvenir shops.

Opening Hours

Local businesses usually open from 8am to 10am and close between 5pm and 7pm weekdays; count on Saturday hours being at least from 10am to 2pm, and on many places being closed Sunday. That said, hours vary a lot: smaller outlets prefer later starts and earlier finishes to the bigger places; shops open an hour or two longer during the warmer months; and businesses in central Prague generally keep longer hours than their suburban counterparts.

Department stores tend to be open from 9am to 8pm weekdays, and from 10am to 6pm on weekends.

TAX FREE...BUT NOT FOR EU

Foreigners, apart from other EU citizens, can rid themselves of up to 19% value-added tax (VAT) by following a few worthwhile tips.

Buy goods worth at least 2000Kč from a shop displaying a 'Tax Free Shopping' sign. When handing over your cash/plastic, ask for a tax-free shopping cheque (to be filled out in the shop with your name and address). Leave the Czech Republic within 90 days from date of purchase and get the cheque stamped by Czech customs. Finally, head for one of the payment points listed on the ubiquitous *Where to Shop Tax Free – Prague* brochures within six weeks of purchase and get your refund.

DEPARTMENT STORES & SHOPPING MALLS

Debenhams (4, F5)

This huge British department store carries much the same stock, at similar prices, as the multiple UK outlets. Clothes, shoes, homewares, perfumes and toys fill the floors, and there's a branch of the Julius Meinl supermarket in the basement.

☎ 221 015 057 ⊠ Václavské náměstí 21, Nové Město ☺ 9am-9pm Mon-Sat, 10am-8pm Sun Ⓜ Můstek

Tesco goes festive

House of the Black Rose (7, E4)

Pasáž Černá Růže is a three-storey shopping mall where you can pick up a few bottles of fine wine, crystal goblets, baggy surfer shorts, a skateboard and even wigs, if the mood strikes you.
⊠ Na příkopě 12, Nové Město ☺ 9am-8pm Mon-Fri, 9am-7pm Sat, 11am-7pm Sun Ⓜ Můstek

Kotva (7, F1)

Huge, ugly, angular and rather brown mall with five floors of clothes, shoes, sports equipment, toys, electronics, furniture, china, jewellery and glass . There's a chemist (drugstore) on the ground floor, and a subterranean supermarket.
☎ 224 801 111 ⊠ náměstí Republiky 8 ☺ 9am-8pm Mon-Fri, 10am-7pm Sat, 10am-6pm Sun Ⓜ Náměstí Republiky

Nový Smíchov (6, B5)

Prague's biggest and most frenetic shopping mall has over 150 stores, with fashion predominating. The gigantic Carrefour supermarket attracts lengthy queues, and there's a food court, cinema, bars, a bowling alley and video-game arcade.
☎ 251 511 151

⊠ Plženská 8, Smíchov ☺ shops 9am-9pm, entertainment 11am-11pm, supermarket 7am-midnight Ⓜ Anděl

Palác Flóra (6, E4)

This big shiny shopping centre, filled with designer boutiques, 'lifestyle stores' and trendy coffee bars, could be anywhere in the Western world. There's a food court, a couple of decent restaurants and a multiscreen cinema (p93).
☎ 255 741 700 ⊠ Vinohradská 151, Vinohrady ☺ 8am-midnight Ⓜ Flóra

Slovanský Dům (7, F3)

This bright shopping centre houses a 10-screen cinema, a couple of good restaurants and several upmarket fashion outlets. A pleasant open courtyard at the back has a beer garden for the tired and thirsty, and more shops for serial spenders.
☎ 221 451 400 ⌨ www .slovanskydum.cz ⊠ Na příkopě 22, Nové Město ☺ 10am-8pm Ⓜ Náměstí Republiky

Tesco (4, D5)

A vast, multistorey maze stocking everything from toiletries and stationery to kitchenware and clothing.

The ground floor takeaway food section draws a shuffling queue, and there's a huge hectic basement supermarket.
☎ 222 003 111 ✉ Národní 26, Nové Město ⏱ 8am-9pm Mon-Fri, 9am-8pm Sat, 10am-8pm Sun Ⓜ Národní Třída

Vinohradský Pavilion (3, C2)
Set in an imposing 19th-century market hall, this trendy mall has four floors of brand-name fashions plus electronics, jewellery, household goods and a dry-cleaner. There's also a supermarket and café.
☎ 222 097 111 ✉ Vinohradská 50, Vinohrady ⏱ 9.30am-9pm Mon-Sat, 10am- 8pm Sun Ⓜ Jiřího z Poděbrad

CLOTHING & ACCESSORIES

Bata (4, E5)
There are seven floors worth of shoes to peruse at this flagship store of the Czech

Czech out the locally designed fashions

footwear retailer, including international brands such as Diesel, Vagabond and Cat, as well as Bata's own. Luggage, handbags and clothes are also to be found.
☎ 224 218 133 ✉ Václavské náměstí 6, Nové Město ⏱ 9am-9pm Mon-Fri, 9am-8pm Sat, 10am-8pm Sun Ⓜ Můstek

Boheme (7, C1)
Showcases the designs of Hana Stocklassa and her associates, with collections of knitwear, leather and suede garments for women. Suede skirts, linen blouses and sweaters seem to be the

stock in trade, and there's also a range of jewellery.
☎ 224 813 840 🖳 www .boheme.cz ✉ Dušní 8, Nové Město ⏱ 10am-7pm Mon-Fri, 11am-4pm Sat Ⓜ Staroměstská

Bushman (4, D6)
If you're thinking of heading off into the bush, come here first. Australian-style outdoor wear includes wax jackets, chinos, T-shirts and bush hats.
☎ 224 948 010 🖳 www .bushmanwear.com ✉ Lazarská 5, Nové Město ⏱ 9.30am-6.30pm Mon-Fri, 10am-3pm Sat Ⓜ Národní Třída

CLOTHING & SHOE SIZES

Women's Clothing
Aust/UK	8	10	12	14	16	18
Europe	36	38	40	42	44	46
Japan	5	7	9	11	13	15
USA	6	8	10	12	14	16

Women's Shoes
Aust/USA	5	6	7	8	9	10
Europe	35	36	37	38	39	40
France only	35	36	38	39	40	42
Japan	22	23	24	25	26	27
UK	3½	4½	5½	6½	7½	8½

Men's Clothing
Aust	92	96	100	104	108	112
Europe	46	48	50	52	54	56

Japan	S	M	M		L	
UK/USA	35	36	37	38	39	40

Men's Shirts (Collar Sizes)
Aust/Japan	38	39	40	41	42	43
Europe	38	39	40	41	42	43
UK/USA	15	15½	16	16½	17	17½

Men's Shoes
Aust/UK	7	8	9	10	11	12
Europe	41	42	43	44½	46	47
Japan	26	27	27.5	28	29	30
USA	7½	8½	9½	10½	11½	12½

Measurements approximate only; try before you buy.

Dunhill (7, C1)

Nothing to wear to that social event of the season? Then you'll probably find what you need in this upmarket British fashion house, with its wide selection of men's casual and formal wear. While you're there you can also take a look through the watches, wallets and fragrances.

✉ Pařížská třída 14, Josefov ⏰ 10am-7pm Mon-Fri, 11am-5pm Sat & Sun Ⓜ Staroměstská

Helena Fejková Gallery (4, F5)

Kit yourself out in the latest Czech fashions at this boutique and showroom. Contemporary men's and women's clothing and accessories by leading Czech designer Helena Fejková and others are on display. Private fashion shows can also be arranged.

☎ 224 211 514 🖥 www .helenafejkova.cz ✉ Lucerna Passage, Štěpánská 61, Nové Město ⏰ 10am-7pm Mon-Fri, 10am-3pm Sat Ⓜ Muzeum

Ivana Follová (7, D1)

She's still standing – Prague designer Ivana Follová specialises in colourful hand-painted silk dresses, many of which can be seen at this boutique. Only natural materials are used in her creations, and accessories, such as handmade glass beads, are also on show.

☎ 224 895 460 🖥 www .ifart.cz ✉ Týnský dvůr 1, Staré Město ⏰ 10.30am-7pm Ⓜ Náměstí Republiky

Klara Nademlýnská (7, D1)

Klara Nademlýnská is one of the Czech Republic's top designers, and you can pick up some stylish women's wear at this little shop. Evening gowns, suits, blouses and swimwear can be had.

☎ 224 818 769 ✉ Dlouhá 3, Staré Město ⏰ 10am-6pm Mon-Fri, 11am-6pm Sat Ⓜ Staroměstská

Marks & Spencer (4, F5)

The British fashion store stocks its signature range of smart casual and more formal clothing, including an entire floor for lingerie. There's also small selection of wine and foodstuff (of the shortbread and teabags variety) and a café.

☎ 224 237 503 ✉ Vá-clavské náměstí 36, Nové Město ⏰ 9.30am-8pm Mon-Fri, 10am-7pm Sat, 10.30am-7pm Sun Ⓜ Můstek

Promod (4, E4)

Big, bright and bold women's wear store – one of five branches in the city – with two floors of trendy, youthful fashion for the stylish girl about town. Shoes, handbags and other assorted accessories are sold here too.

☎ 296 327 701 ✉ Václav-ské náměstí 2, Nové Město ⏰ 10am-9pm Mon-Sat, noon-7pm Sun Ⓜ Můstek

Senior Bazar (4, G4)

Popular secondhand clothing outlet, with plenty of bargains to be found among the racks. Vintage dresses, suits, jeans and more recent castaways are all in search of a new home.

☎ 224 235 068 ✉ Senovážné náměstí 18, Nové Město ⏰ 9am-5pm Mon-Fri Ⓜ Náměstí Republiky

JEWELLERY

Český Granát Turnov (4, E2)

Reputedly the biggest creator of Bohemian garnet jewellery, Granát Turnov offers silver and gold rings, brooches, cuff links and necklaces showing off the unique blood-red stones. Less expensive adornments comprising the dark green, semiprecious stone *vltavín* are also on sale.

☎ 222 315 612 🖥 www .granat-cz.com ✉ Dlouhá 30, Josefov ⏰ 10am-6pm Mon-Sat, 10am-1pm Sun Ⓜ Náměstí Republiky

Fabergé (7, B1)

The jewellers to the Tsars certainly know how to put on the most mesmerising

GRAB A GARNET

The blood-red stone that you'll see dangling off the wrists and necks of Prague's populace is more than likely one of the more colourful versions of the Czech garnet *(český granát)*, a popular urban accessory and an even more popular tourist purchase. Garnets aren't always red – some are almost colourless and others are black, while the scarce green garnet is much sought-after. According to traditional rumours (often embellished by retailers) the gemstone consistently wields its mystical powers to replace sadness with joy.

displays. This gorgeously stocked store has their trademark Easter-egg pendants, as well as sparkly rings, cuff links, brooches and other top-end ornaments.

☎ 222 323 639 ⊠ Pařížská 15, Josefov ⏲ 10am-8pm Ⓜ Staroměstská

Galerie Vlasta (7, C2)
This small boutique showcases the contemporary delicate gold and silver wire jewellery of award-winning Czech designer Vlasta Wasserbaurová. There's a dazzling array of highly distinctive net-like brooches, necklaces and earrings on display.

☎ 222 318 119 ⊠ Staroměstské náměstí 5, Staré Město ⏲ 10am-6pm Mon-Fri, 10am-1pm Sat Ⓜ Staroměstská

Lavie (4, D2)
Specialising in brilliant diamonds, in all shapes, sizes and hues, Lavie also has a selection of other mounted precious stones. There's another branch with delightful jewellery at Palác Flóra (p54).

☎ 224 811 011 🖳 www .laviejewellery.com

⊠ Maiselova 21, Josefov ⏲ 10am-6pm Sun-Fri Ⓜ Staroměstská

U České orlice (7, E2)
Elegant traditional Czech jewellery, including lots of garnets and chunky amber, as well as more restrained pieces in gold and silver. Exquisite, hand-painted porcelain and other *objets d'art* fill the shop.

☎ 224 228 544 ⊠ Celetná 30, Staré Město ⏲ 10am-8pm Ⓜ Náměstí Republiky

U Klementina (7, B3)
Look over some beautiful gold, silver, amber and garnet jewellery and a range of designer watches at this welcoming store. Well-

informed staff are happy to show you around.

☎ 222 220 240 ⊠ Karlova 22, Staré Město ⏲ 10am-midnight Ⓜ Staroměstská

ARTS & CRAFTS

Art Décoratif (7, F2)
Beautiful reproductions of fine Art Nouveau and Art Deco glassware, jewellery and fabrics are sold here. You'll also find the gorgeously delicate glass creations by Jarmila Plockova, granddaughter of Alfons Mucha, who has been inspired by his paintings.

☎ 220 002 350 ⊠ U Obecního domu, Staré Město ⏲ 10am-8pm Ⓜ Náměstí Republiky

Bohemia Crystal (7, E3)
One of several city outlets for Bohemia Crystal's considerable range of glassware, ranging from the functional to the fantastic. Champagne flutes, whisky tumblers and purely ornamental pieces are on show.
☎ 224 239 653 ✉ Napřikopě 17, Nové Město
🕑 10am-8pm Ⓜ Můstek

Celetná Crystal (7, E2)
This vast, sparkling emporium has a dazzling range of traditional and contemporary cut crystal laid out over three levels. Whether it's martini glasses, crystal pineapples, chandeliers or any other glassy luxury you're looking for, you are most likely to find it here. Bohemian porcelain and amber jewellery are there to tempt you.
☎ 222 324 022 🖳 www .czechcrystal.com ✉ Celetná 15, Staré Město 🕑 10am-10pm Ⓜ Náměstí Republiky

Galerie Pyramida (4, C5)
Wonderfully original art, sculpture and striking glass by contemporary Czech artists are on display here. This being Prague, the element of Surrealism is never far away and many pieces have more than a touch of the psychedelic fantasy about them.
☎ 224 213 1 17 ✉ Národní třída 11, Nové Město 🕑 10.30am-7pm Ⓜ Národní Třída

Gallery of Surrealism (7, A3)
Eye-catching little gallery showcasing the bizarre imaginings of Prague artist Viktor Safonkin (think Salvador Dalí meets Hieronymus Bosch). Though Safonkin's paintings command huge prices, and small prints of his works go for around 2500Kč, it's still worth a quick browse.
☎ 222 220 696 🖳 www .eurosurrealism.com

✉ Karlova 12, Staré Město
🕑 11am-7pm Ⓜ Národní Třída

Krámek U Škopků (4, B3)
This small shop sells a dazzling selection of handmade reproduction glassware and ceramics, based on medieval and Renaissance designs. Raise a goblet to the knights of old!
☎ 257 531 926 🖳 www .bohemart.cz ✉ U lužického semináře 22, Malá Strana
🕑 11am-8pm
Ⓜ Malostranská

Kubista (7, E2)
In the House of the Black Madonna, this shop specialises in surprisingly expensive reproductions of Cubist ceramics by Pavel Janák, as seen in the Museum of Czech Cubism (p17). It also sells a few books and some original pieces of furniture for serious collectors with serious cash.
☎ 224 236 378 🖳 www .kubista.cz ✉ Ovocný trh 19, Staré Město 🕑 10am-6pm Ⓜ Náměstí Republiky

Manufactura (7, C3)
Multibranch store selling a huge assortment of traditional Czech handicrafts, including wooden toys, scented soaps, beeswax candles, gingerbread ornaments, ceramics, linen and colourful, hand-painted *kraslice* (Easter eggs), which carry a variety of regional designs.
☎ 221 632 480 🖳 www .manufactura.biz ✉ Melantrichova 17, Staré Město
🕑 10am- 7pm Mon-Thu, 10am-7.30pm Fri-Sun
Ⓜ Můstek

Surrealist art takes many shapes and forms in Prague

Easter eggs of the non-fattening *kraslice* kind

Rott Crystal (7, B3)
Rott's vibrant *sgraffito*-covered (multilayered mural) façade dates from its previous incarnation as an ironmonger's. Today it shows off traditional and contemporary crystal creations, as well as garnet jewellery and porcelain.
☎ 224 229 529 ✉ Malé náměstí 3, Staré Město ☺ 10am-10pm Ⓜ Staroměstská

U Dominikánů (7, B3)
This friendly gallery sells paintings and ceramics by contemporary Prague artists. The artists occasionally mill around and are happy to discuss their work.
☎ 608 049 648 ✉ Jilská 7a, Staré Město ☺ 11am-6pm Ⓜ Staroměstská

ANTIQUES & BRIC-A-BRAC

Antik v Dlouhé (4, F2)
Those with some spare time on their hands might enjoy a rummage through the 19th-century clutter in this curiosity shop. Among the junk there are some wonderful ceramics, jewellery and paintings, as well as the odd teddy bear, chandelier and mantle clock.

☎ 224 826 347 ✉ Dlouhá 37, Josefov ☺ 10am-6pm Mon-Fri, 10am-3pm Sat Ⓜ Náměstí Republiky

Antique Ahasver (5, C4)
This little shop is one big jumble of old lace – lots and lots of lace – everything from doilies to tablecloths. There's also a good collection of vintage dresses and the odd bits of jewellery and assorted knick-knacks.
☎ 257 531 404 ✉ Prokopská 3, Malá Strana ☺ 11am-6pm Tue-Sun Ⓜ Malostranská, then tram 12, 22, 23 or 57

Antique Music Instruments (2, A2)
It might not get the prize for Prague's most inventive shop name, but this place is a real treasure trove of vintage stringed, brass and woodwind instruments.
☎ 233 353 779 🖳 www.antiques.cz ✉ Pohořelec 9, Hradčany ☺ 9am-6pm Ⓜ Malostranská, then tram 22 or 23 to Pohořelec

Art Deco (5, B3)
All things 1930s are the rage at this engaging, if tiny, boutique. There's lots of silver and glass on display, as well as some fashionable jewellery, both original and

reproduction, and stunning Czech glass and porcelain from the Jazz Age.
☎ 257 535 801 ✉ Jánský vršek 8, Malá Strana ☺ noon-7pm Mon-Fri, 11am-7pm Sat & Sun Ⓜ Malostranská, then tram 12, 22, 23 or 57 to Malostranské náměstí

Art Deco Galerie (7, C3)
Unrelated to the Art Deco shop, this place has a larger selection of 1920s and '30s style, including some striking dresses and hats. China, glass and jewellery fill the store, along with knick-knacks such as cigarette cases of the sort Bertie Wooster might have flourished.
☎ 224 223 076 ✉ Michalská 21, Staré Město ☺ 2-7pm Mon-Fri Ⓜ Můstek

Art Deco in the window...

Bric-à-Brac (7, D1)
There's barely room to move through the accumulation of random junk in this overstuffed shop. Old typewriters, perfume bottles, prints, dolls, teacups, puppets and hats litter every surface. One glance at the outrageous price tickets and you'll realise why stock remains so abundant.
☎ 224 815 763 ☒ Týnská 7, Staré Město ☽ 10am-7pm Ⓜ Náměstí Republiky

Dorotheum (7, E3)
Venerable, upmarket gallery and auction house founded in 1707, and specialising in exquisite 19th- and early-20th-century glassware, porcelain, fine art and furniture. Auctions are held at infrequent intervals; check the website for details.
☎ 224 222 001 🖳 www .dorotheum.cz ☒ Ovocný trh 2, Staré Město ☽ 10am-7pm Mon-Fri, 10am-5pm Sat Ⓜ Náměstí Republiky

Eduard Čapek (4, E2-F2)
The Čapek clan have lovingly operated their bric-a-brac shop since 1911 and nothing has ever been thrown away, including the dust. Rolls of recycled electrical wire, rusty tools, dog-eared magazines and battered handbags are among the...er...treasures awaiting your perusal.
☒ Dlouhá 32, Josefov ☽ 10am-6pm Mon-Fri Ⓜ Náměstí Republiky

Icons Gallery (2, A2)
In the same building as Antique Music Instruments (p59), this cluttered little shop has a luminous selection of Russian and Eastern European icons, as well as numerous other decorative *objets d'art*, watches, porcelain and Art Nouveau glassware.
☎ 233 353 777 ☒ Pohořelec 9, Hradčany ☽ 9am-6pm Ⓜ Malostranská, then tram 22 or 23 to Pohořelec

MUSIC

AghaRTA Jazz Centrum (7, D3)
Inside the esteemed AghaRTA club is a selection of the best Czech and world jazz CDs for the purist to ponder over. Pick up some Miles Davis and Chet Baker, or try 'The Best of AghaRTA' compilation album, featuring contemporary Prague performers.
☎ 222 211 275 ☒ Železná 16, Staré Město ☽ 7pm-midnight Mon-Thu, 8pm-midnight Fri-Sun Ⓜ Můstek

Andante Music (5, C3)
This small shop specialising in classical music CDs has most of the big names covered, with a comprehensive collection of Czech and foreign composers. It also sells tickets to classical music concerts in town.
☎ 257 533 718 ☒ Mostecká 26, Malá Strana ☽ 10am-6pm Ⓜ Malostranská

Bontonland (4, E4)
Purportedly the biggest music megastore in the Czech Republic, this place covers pretty much everything, including Western chart music, classical, jazz, dance and heavy metal, as well as an extensive collection of Czech pop. It also sells DVDs and video games.
☎ 224 473 080 🖳 www .bontonland.cz ☒ Palác Koruna, Václavské náměstí 1, Nové Město ☽ 9am-8pm Mon-Sat, 10am-7pm Sun Ⓜ Můstek

Music Antiquariat (4, D5)
Browse through some of the thousands of new and

Eduard Čapek awaits

So many titles, so little time

secondhand rock 'n' roll, pop, jazz, classical and blues LPs and CDs in this upstairs store. Most prominent is the extensive vinyl collection, where you can find everything from Max Bygraves to Metallica.
☎ 221 085 268 ✉ level 1, Palác Metro, Národní třída 25, Nové Město ⏲ 10.30am-7pm Mon-Sat Ⓜ Národní Třída

Philharmonia (7, C1)
Sample the classics at Philharmonia, including the many works of Dvořák, Janáček and Smetana. Jazz, blues, Czech folk, Jewish music and more can also be found.
☎ 224 811 258 ✉ Pařížská třída 13, Josefov ⏲ 10am-6pm Ⓜ Staroměstská

Via Musica (5, B3)
On the ground floor of the Liechtenstein Palace, Via Musica stocks a good selection of classical, jazz and Jewish music and sells tickets for concerts around Prague. There's another, smaller branch just off Staroměstské náměstí (7, D2).
☎ 257 535 568 🖳 www.viamusica. cz ✉ Malostranské náměstí 13, Malá Strana ⏲ 10.30am-12.30pm & 1-7pm Ⓜ Malostranská

BOOKS

Academia Bookshop (4, F5)
Czech-language academic and scientific tomes dominate the upper floors of this big book shop, while downstairs you can leaf through English novels, travel guides and lots of maps and books about Prague.
☎ 224 223 511 ✉ Václavské náměstí 34, Nové Město ⏲ 9am-8pm Mon-Fri, 9.30am-7pm Sat, 9.30am-6pm Sun Ⓜ Můstek

Anagram (7, D2-E2)
This popular English-language bookshop has a big selection of novels and nonfiction, covering subjects such as European history, philosophy, religion, art and travel. There are also Lonely Planet titles, Czech novels, children's books and a section of secondhand titles.
☎ 224 895 737 🖳 www .anagram.cz ✉ Týnský dvůr 4, Staré Město ⏲ 10am-8pm Mon-Sat, 10am-6pm Sun Ⓜ Náměstí Republiky

Antikvariát (7, D2)
Antiquarian bookshop with a sizable stock of mostly Czech and German titles, on a wide variety of topics. It also stocks an interesting collection of old prints, aquatints and maps to browse through.
☎ 224 895 775 ✉ Týnský dvůr 2, Staré Město ⏲ 10am-7pm Ⓜ Náměstí Republiky

CLASSICAL SOUNDS
Prague is truly a city with music in its heart. Mozart, Haydn, Tchaikovsky and other greats were all frequent visitors. Mozart even named one of his symphonies after Prague and conducted the premiere of his opera *Don Giovanni* at the Estates Theatre. Sons of whom Prague is justly proud include Antonín Dvořák, the best internationally recognised Czech composer, and Bedřich Smetana, whose *Má Vlast* (My Homeland) opens the Prague Spring festival each year. Both are honoured with museums in the city. The music of Bohuslav Martinů and Moravian-born Leoš Janáček is also played and loved the world over.

Big Ben (7, E1)
Well-stocked English-language bookshop, with shelves devoted to Prague reference books, travel, children's literature, science fiction, poetry and the latest bestsellers. Various magazines and newspapers are also at hand.
☎ 224 826 565 ✉ Malá Štupartská 5, Staré Město
🕙 9am-6.30pm Mon-Fri, 10am-5pm Sat & Sun
Ⓜ Náměstí Republiky

Browsing for books at Anagram

Fraktaly (4, D4)
This overflowing bookshop boasts an assortment of titles in English and Czech, on architecture, design, art, photography and associated topics, as well as English-language periodicals.
☎ 222 222 186 ✉ Betlémské náměstí 5a, Staré Město
🕙 10am-9pm Ⓜ Národní Třída

Globe (4, C6)
Popular hang-out for book-hunting backpackers, with a quiet café in which to peruse your purchases. There's lots of new fiction and nonfiction and English magazines, plus a big selection of secondhand novels.
☎ 224 934 203 ✉ Pštrossova 6, Nové Město
🕙 10am-midnight Ⓜ Karlovo Náměstí

Palác Knih Neo Luxor (4, F5)
Prague's biggest bookshop sells multifarious novels in English, German, French and other languages, including Czech authors in translation. A whole section is devoted to books about Prague and there's a good selection of Lonely Planet guides, maps, international magazines and newspapers.
☎ 221 111 364 🖳 www .neoluxor.cz ✉ Václavské náměstí 41, Nové Město
🕙 8am-8pm Mon-Fri, 9am-7pm Sat, 10am-7pm Sun Ⓜ Můstek

U Černé Matky Boží Knihkupectví (7, E2)
Located on the ground floor of the House of the Black Madonna, this touristy bookshop has a big assemblage of books on the Czech Republic and Prague, as well as children's books and translations of Kafka, Hrabel, Hašek et al in English, French, German, Spanish and Italian.
☎ 224 222 239 ✉ Celetná 34, Staré Město 🕙 9.30am-7pm Mon-Fri, 10am-7pm Sat & Sun Ⓜ Náměstí Republiky

TALES FROM THE CITY

Prague has fuelled the imagination of many Czech authors and literary visitors. Towering above them all is Franz Kafka, whose smothering, angst-ridden fantasies, as explored in *The Metamorphosis, The Castle* and *The Trial,* have been shuddered over in all corners of the world. Gustav Meyrink put a suitably dark spin on the city's favourite legend in *The Golem,* while another Czech preferring the less-lit path is Milan Kundera, who set *The Unbearable Lightness of Being* here.

But Czech literature isn't all paranoia, nightmares and giant beetles. Jaroslav Hašek wrote one of the Czechs' best-loved novels, *The Good Soldier Švejk,* a comical tale following the misadventures of a boozy WWI squaddie. Karel Čapek, meanwhile, introduced the word 'robot' into the English language in his sci-fi classic, *RUR.*

FOOD & DRINK

Albio (4, G2)
Organic and 'green' products fill this minimarket, where, among other things, you can pick up fruit and veg, tea, wine and fresh bread. It's under the same management as the nearby restaurant Albio (p71).
☎ 222 325 418 ⌨ www .albiostyl.cz ✉ Truhlářská 18, Nové Město ☼ 8am-8pm Mon-Fri, 9am-5pm Sat Ⓜ Náměstí Republiky

Cellarius (4, F5)
Countless fine wines from across the globe are on sale here, with the Czech Republic best represented. There are seats outside where you can enjoy a glass or two of a good Frankovka or Müller Thurgau while gazing up at David Černý's topsy-turvy St Wenceslas statue.
☎ 224 210 979 ⌨ www .cellarius.cz ✉ Lucerna Passage, Štěpánská 61, Nové Město ☼ 9.30am-9pm Mon-Sat, 3-8pm Sun Ⓜ Muzeum

Country Life (7, C3)
Attached to the neighbouring vegetarian restaurant (p75), this minimarket sells a good range of healthy organic fare, from teas and tonics to soy sausages, honey and cereals.
☎ 224 213 366 ✉ Melant-richova 15, Staré Město ☼ 8.30am-7pm Mon-Thu, 8.30am-6pm Fri, 11am-6pm Sun Ⓜ Můstek

Fruits de France (4, F5)
Gallic gastronomes and Francophile foodies will make a beeline for this consumables shop and its stash of fine wines, cheeses, vegetables and all manner of fresh, canned and bottled French fare.
☎ 224 220 304 ✉ Jindřišská 9, Nové Město ☼ 9.30am-6.30pm Mon-Fri, 9.30am-1pm Sat Ⓜ Můstek

Havelská Market (7, C4)
Hurry past the tacky souvenir stalls that dominate bustling Havelská Market and instead check out the mountains of fresh fruit and veg, and tasty treats such as homemade gingerbread.
✉ Havelská, Staré Město ☼ 8am-6pm Ⓜ Můstek

La Casa de Cigarros y del Vino (7, E4)
Hidden inside the Černá Růže shopping centre, this aromatic shop sells quality international wines, from both well-established producers and more unusual sources, including Israel, Romania and, of course, the Czech Republic. Cigars are also abundant.
☎ 221 014 716 ✉ Na příkopě 12, Nové Město ☼ 9am-8pm Mon-Fri, 9am-7pm Sat, 11am-7pm Sun Ⓜ Můstek

Sapori Italiani (4, D5)
Those longing for a taste of Italy should find satisfaction in this delicatessen, with its fine stock of Italian wines, cheeses and meats. Pasta and tasty sauces are available, along with other tinned and bottled goods.
☎ 224 234 952 ✉ Perlová 10, Nové Město ☼ 10am-7pm Mon-Fri, 11am-5pm Sat & Sun Ⓜ Můstek

Tempt your tastebuds with Albio's organic restaurant

FOR CHILDREN

Art Dekor (7, E3)
This charmingly old-fashioned store overflows with handmade stuffed animals, in a variety of colourful fabrics that are sure to delight any toddler. So, whether it's a green teddy, a cat covered in blue sailing boats or a batik elephant you have in mind, call in here.
☎ 221 637 178 ✉ Ovocný trh 12, Nové Město
🕑 10am-7pm Mon-Sat, 10am-6pm Sun Ⓜ Můstek

Hračky U Zlatého Iva (7, E2)
It's marionettes galore in this toyshop, brimming with hundreds of puppets, from fairytale favourites to more modern figures such as Harry Potter and, rather curiously, Sigmund Freud. Upstairs there's an assortment of simple wooden toys and dolls. The proliferation of 'Don't Touch' signs seems rather optimistic however.
☎ 224 239 469 ✉ Celetná 32, Staré Město 🕑 9am-8pm Ⓜ Náměstí Republiky

Mothercare (7, E3)
If you're travelling with a baby or toddler, you'll find pretty much everything you need to meet their nonedible demands here. Toys, clothes, prams, cots, maternity wear and other goods for mother and child are at hand.
☎ 222 240 008 🖥 www .mothercare.cz ✉ Pasáž Myselbek, Nové Město
🕑 9.30am-8pm Mon-Fri, 9am-7pm Sat, 11am-6pm Sun Ⓜ Náměstí Republiky

Sparkys (7, D3)
Prague's biggest toyshop has four floors of playthings to entrance younger visitors and to part their parents from their cash. Traditional wooden toys, stuffed animals, model cars, computer games, board games and cartoon videos and DVDs are there to be had.
☎ 221 411 312 🖥 www .sparkys.cz ✉ Havířská 2, Staré Město 🕑 10am-7pm Ⓜ Můstek

SPECIALIST STORES

Baker Street (7, F2)
Selling racks of beautifully

Irrestitible Czech mates

made, brightly polished pipes, Baker Street also has a range of cigars and some snazzy lighters. On top of that, you can also stock up on superstrong absinthe here too. Fuggy nights await…
☎ 224 231 117 ✉ Celetná 38, Staré Město 🕑 10am-8pm Mon-Sat, 10am-6pm Sun Ⓜ Náměstí Republiky

Botanicus (7, D1)
Prepare for olfactory overload in this busy outlet for natural beauty products and organic condiments. The mountain of scented soaps always draws a crowd of sniffers, and you can rummage through shelves laden with herbal bath oils, shampoos, lotions, fruit cordials, chutneys and flavoured vinegars.
☎ 224 895 445 ✉ Týnský dvůr 3, Staré Město
🕑 10am-8pm
Ⓜ Náměstí Republiky

Boulder Shop (4, E6)
In the same building as Boulder Bar (p83), this little store sells a jumble of outdoorsy accessories such

---

MARKET DAY
Prague has a few open-air markets to scatter money around, most of them open daily (some closed Sunday) from early morning to dusk. The most prominent is the food and souvenir market on **Havelská** (7, C4), which started life as a collective of specialist markets for German merchants around 1230.

Less-distinguished markets, where cheap clothes elbow mounds of perfume, alcohol and toys, include the stalls at **Florenc** (4, J2), the vendors near Hradčanská metro at **Dejvice** (6, B3), and the commercial sprawl at **Bubenské nábřeží** (6, D2).

as walking shoes, socks, fleeces, backpacks, shorts and T-shirts.
☎ 222 231 253 ✉ V jámě 6, Nové Město ✦ 10am-7pm Mon-Fri, 10am-4pm Sat & Sun Ⓜ Můstek

Cat's Gallery (7, D2)

If you like cats, you'll love Cat's Gallery, with its colourful collection of feline ephemera. Cat-emblazoned T-shirts, cups, calendars and clocks can all be had, or perhaps you're searching for an anthropomorphic ceramic cat smoking a cigar? Look no further!
✉ Týnská ulička 9, Staré Město ✦ 10am-7pm Ⓜ Náměstí Republiky

Centrum Foto Škoda (4, E5)

This gigantic camera store has a healthy stock of professional photographic equipment and accessories, telescopes and binoculars. It also sells vintage cameras, and there's a processing lab on site.
☎ 222 929 029 🖳 www .fotoskoda.cz ✉ Palác Langhans, Vodičkova 37, Nové Město ✦ 8.30am-8pm Mon-Fri, 9am-6pm Sat, noon-6.30pm Sun Ⓜ Můstek

Donate (7, E4)

Upstairs in the 'Black Rose' shopping centre, Donate specialises in attractive garden furniture, and other outdoor oddments including garden lamps, hammocks, cushions, candles, picnic sets and crockery.
☎ 221 014 446 🖳 www .donate.cz ✉ 2nd floor, Pasáž Černá Růže, Na Příkopě 12, Nové Město ✦ 10am-

8pm Mon-Fri, 10am-7pm Sat, 11am-7pm Sun Ⓜ Můstek

Karel Vávra (3, A3)

Handmade fiddles decorate the interior of this old-fashioned violin workshop, where Karel and his assistants beaver away making and repairing the instruments in a time-honoured fashion. Even if you're not in search of a custom-made violin, it's worth a look just for the atmosphere.
☎ 222 518 114 🖳 www.housle-vavra.cz ✉ Lublaňská 65, Vinohrady ✦ 9am-5pm Ⓜ IP Pavlova

Le Patio Lifestyle (4, D2)

An engaging clutter of furniture, glass, china, 'ethnic' carvings and stylish homeware accessories can be found at Le Patio. There's an intriguing clutter of oddments to browse through, spread over two rooms.
☎ 222 320 260 ✉ Pařížská 20, Josefov ✦ 10am-7pm Mon-Sat, 11am-7pm Sun Ⓜ Staroměstská

Minerály Praha (7, D2)

Located down a little shopping arcade off Celetná, this interesting outlet has

a display of crystals and minerals from around the world, as well as a selection of handmade jewellery.
☎ 224 234 573 ✉ Hrzánská Pasáž, Celetná 12, Staré Město ✦ 10am-7pm Ⓜ Staroměstská

Perské Koberce U Mánesa (6, C4)

Handmade carpets and rugs from Iran, Afghanistan, India and elsewhere fill this store room. Colourful pieces come in all sizes and prices, in intricate traditional designs, and the knowledgeable staff can help you make an informed purchase.
☎ 272 735 226 ✉ Myslíkova 3, Nové Město ✦ 10am-6pm Mon-Fri, 10am-3pm Sat Ⓜ Karlovo náměstí

Sanu-Babu (7, C3)

Sandalwood-scented hippie heaven, selling all manner of far out New Age essentials, including incense sticks and holders, bongs, handmade Nepalese paper, wooden carvings and a colourful range of Nepalese clothes.
☎ 221 632 401 🖳 www .sanubabu.cz ✉ Michalská 20, Staré Město ✦ 10.30am-10.30pm Ⓜ Můstek

Lather up with herbal lotions at Botanicus

Eating

Whatever tickles your palette, you'll probably find it in Prague, with restaurants offering everything from the finest French and Italian cuisine to Afghan, Japanese, Colombian, Brazilian and Scandinavian. The standard Czech fare of roast meat and stodgy bread dumplings sometimes gets a bad press, but when it's done well, traditional Czech cuisine can be very tasty. There are plenty of restaurants and pubs serving top-quality local food, or excellent gourmet establishments creatively adapting it with a fresh international approach in mind.

MEAL COSTS

The prices in this chapter indicate the cost of a two-course meal with one drink for one person.

€	up to 260Kč
€€	260–479Kč
€€€	480–750Kč
€€€€	over 750Kč

The average Czech day includes a breakfast (*snídaně*) of coffee with bread (*chléb*), cheese, ham and eggs, eaten at home or at one of the many simple *bufety* (self-service eateries). Lunch (*oběd*) or dinner (*večeře*) consists of soup (*polévka*) and often the ubiquitous dumplings (*knedlo*), sauerkraut (*zelo*) and roast pork (*vepřo*). Other favoured items, particularly in pubs, include pork sausages (*buřt*) and goulash (*guláš*). Pretzels are often found on pub tables – you'll be charged when you leave for what you take.

Service in restaurants has improved greatly in recent years, and the sour-faced indifference and grunts that once characterised Prague waiters are thankfully on the way out, though scattered bastions of grumpiness do remain. Czechs are fond of the old nicotine, and cigarette smoke regularly clouds most establishments, except at lunchtime when the custom is to refrain until lunch is finished. Some places have banning notices up at this time of day.

A place calling itself a *restaurace* should be a cheaper restaurant, but often isn't. A *vinárna* is a wine bar that will mainly serve bite-sized items. A *kavárna* is a café, which in Prague usually means alcohol prevails as much as coffee, and food is restricted to snacks. Restaurant hours vary markedly, as do *kavárna* opening times, with many in the centre staying open late most nights; pubs are usually open from 11am to 11pm.

First, find a table

HRADČANY

Jídelní Lístek (2, A2)
Modern Czech €
No-frills local hang-out with a sociable bar and eclectic menu. Snacks, such as fried mushrooms with cheese, jostle with more substantial dishes such as pork and cabbage, and fried carp.
☎ 220 516 731 ✉ Pohořelec 10 ⏰ 11am-8pm Ⓜ Malostranská, then tram 22 or 23 to Pohořelec ♿ Ⓥ

Klášterní Pivovar Strahov (2, A2)
Traditional Czech €€
Though aimed solidly at the passing tourist traffic, this microbrewery and restaurant in the Strahov Monastery compound has a reasonable menu of roast meats, pickled cheese and the like. The house brew, Sveti Norbert (49Kč per 400mL) isn't bad either. Well, they have been brewing here since the 13th century.
☎ 233 353 155 ✉ Strahovské nádvoří 301 ⏰ 11am-8pm Ⓜ Malostranská, then tram 22 or 23 to Pohořelec Ⓥ

Lobkowicz Palace Café (8, F1)
Café €€
Touristy café in the courtyard of the Lobkowicz Palace, with an outdoor decking area and panoramic terrace. Prices, such as 210Kč for a sandwich and 70Kč for a beer are, frankly, a rip-off, but the Palace has a bit more atmosphere than other cafés within the castle walls.

☎ 602 595 998 ✉ Jiřská 3, Prague Castle ⏰ 10am-6pm Ⓜ Malostranská Ⓥ

Malý Buddha (2, B2)
Vegetarian/Asian €
Serving 'traditional temple vegetable food', noodles, fish and lots of teas, this Oriental haven, complete with a Buddhist shrine, is a quiet place to hang out. Various Asian wines and liqueurs are available too.
☎ 220 513 894 ✉ Úvoz 46 ⏰ 1-10.30pm Tue-Sun Ⓜ Malostranská, then tram 22 or 23 to Pohořelec ♿ Ⓥ

Oživlé Dřevo (2, A3)
Modern Czech €€€€
This rustic, cushion-strewn hall, at the base of Strahov Monastery, is the place to try such fancy fare as marinated venison and grilled turbot. The garden terrace has superb views over Prague, though service can be achingly slow.
☎ 220 517 274 ✉ Strahovské nádvoří 1 ⏰ 11am-11pm Ⓜ Malostranská, then tram 22 or 23 to Pohořelec

Peklo (2, A3)
Modern Czech €€€-€€€€
In the monastery compound, this cavern was once the monks' wine cellar. Today the house speciality is trout, straight from the cellar pond, while old favourites such as duck-and-dumplings make an appearance.
☎ 220 516 652 🖥 www.peklo.com ✉ Strahovské nádvoří 1 ⏰ 6pm-midnight Mon, noon-midnight Tue-Sun Ⓜ Malostranská, then tram 22 or 23 to Pohořelec ♿ Ⓥ

U Labutí (2, C1)
Traditional Czech/beer hall €€-€€€
Once home to Tycho Brahe and Johannes Kepler, this grand medieval mansion is today a convivial restaurant and beer hall with a converted stable (complete with troughs for messy eaters). Goulash, pork and dumplings, and venison are on the menu.
☎ 220 511 191 ✉ Hradčanské náměstí 11 ⏰ 10am-10pm Ⓜ Malostranská ♿ Ⓥ

CZECH, PLEASE…
When eating out in Prague, you might sometimes find that your bill ends up costing you more than you had expected, and it's not always clear why. Here are some hints on coping with costs.

Double-check your bill carefully as there are a few people working in Prague's eateries who either failed maths in school or got top marks in the 'overcharging' business elective. Stuff you'd take for granted back home often comes at a price in Prague – wave away items you didn't order or want, such as baskets of bread and, in more touristy places, 'free' drinks. Remember those pretzels displayed on bar tables aren't free either. Finally, cover charges and tips can be included in your final amount.

JOSEFOV

Ariana (4, E2)
Afghan €€
Afghan carpets, photos and knick-knacks give that semi-authentic feel at this little restaurant. Try an Afghan curry or kebab or specialities such as *qabali uzbeki* (minced mutton with rice), while central Asian music wails in the background.
☎ 222 323 438 ✉ Rámová 6 🕐 11am-11pm
Ⓜ Staroměstská

Bakeshop Praha (4, E2)
Café/breakfast €
This welcoming little café is a great place to while away some time over a cappuccino and muffin, while reading the latest issue of *Guardian Weekly* or other papers thoughtfully provided for customers. Good selection of tempting cakes.
☎ 222 316 823 🖥 www.bakeshop.cz ✉ Kozí 1 🕐 7am-7pm
Ⓜ Staroměstská Ⓥ

Chez Marcel (4, E2)
French/breakfast €€
Sit back, sip a *pastis* (aniseed apertif) while Edith Piaf warbles over the sound system and imagine you're on the Left Bank. Salads, omelettes and sandwiches feature, and the latest French papers are magazines and provided.
☎ 222 315 676 ✉ Haštalská 12 🕐 8am-1am Mon-Fri, 9am-1am Sat & Sun Ⓜ Náměstí Republiky
♿ Ⓥ

King Solomon (7, B1)
Kosher €€€€
You're in Josefov, so why not try some Jewish delicacies

In the mood for Afghan at Ariana

such as gefilte fish, carp and chicken soup? There are also inventive recipes involving duck, venison and lamb. Vegetarians won't find much to munch.
☎ 224 818 752 ✉ Široká 8 🕐 noon-11pm Sun-Thu Ⓜ Staroměstská ♿

Lary Fary (4, E2)
Fusion €€€
There are a number of themed rooms in the Lary Fary restaurant, so you can choose to dine under a Buddha, in Moorish surrounds or among Moghul interior décor. The food is equally diverse, with offerings such as beef in Thai marinade and sweet-and-sour duck noodles.
☎ 222 320 154 🖥 www.laryfary.cz ✉ Dlouhá 30 🕐 11am-midnight
Ⓜ Náměstí Republiky

La Bodeguita del Medio (7, A1)
Cuban €€€-€€€€
At this spin-off from Hemingway's favourite haunt in Havana, there's a noisy bar upstairs while downstairs the restaurant serves Cuban and Creole cuisine. Grilled prawns, fried octopus and

lobster are offered, while live music, Cuban cigars and ceiling fans complete the scene.
☎ 224 813 922 🖥 www.bodeguita.cz ✉ Kaprova 5 🕐 10am-2am Ⓜ Staroměstská

La Scène (4, E2)
French €€€€
A Michelin-starred chef prepares some of Prague's best French cuisine at chic La Scène. Snail ragout, red mullet soufflé and lamb fillet with gingerbread crust grace the menu, and there's also a more casual café-wine bar and an artfully styled 'champagne club' downstairs.
☎ 222 312 677 🖥 www.lascene.cz ✉ U milosrdných 6 🕐 restaurant noon-2pm & 7-11pm, café 8am-midnight, champagne club 8pm-2am Ⓜ Staroměstská

Les Moules (4, D2)
Belgian/café €€
This 'Belgian Beer Café' provides an authentic brasserie atmosphere for typical cuisine such as the eponymous mussels, *pommes frites*, and seafood dishes including octopus salad. The bar stocks 25 mostly Belgian beers.

☎ 222 315 022 ▢ www
.lesmoules.cz ✉ Pařížská
třída 19 ☽ 9am-midnight
Ⓜ Staroměstská

Nostress (4, D2)
Fusion €€€-€€€€
Ultra fashionable French-
Asian 'fusion' restaurant
planted with a small
forest of bamboo. 'Thai
style *bouillabaisse*', beef
curry with peanuts and
roast salmon figure on the
menu, and there's a bar
and separate furnishings
gallery.
☎ 222 317 004 ▢ www
.nostress.cz ✉ Dušní 10
☽ 8am-11pm Mon-Fri,
10am-11pm Sat & Sun
Ⓜ Staroměstská

Orange Moon (4, E2)
Southeast Asian €€
Bright orange walls, paper
lanterns and Asian photos
provide the perfect ambi-
ence for the Thai, Burmese
and Indian cuisines served
here. Clear your sinuses with
some of the spicier curry
options; the menu provides
an accurate chilli index to
select your own level of spice
comfort. There's also an 89Kč
set-lunch menu.
☎ 222 325 119 ▢ www
.orangemoon.cz ✉ Rám-
ová 5 ☽ 11.30am-11.30pm
Ⓜ Staroměstská Ⓥ

Pravda (4, D2)
Fusion €€€-€€€€
Fashionable dining on
Prague's ultrastylish
thoroughfare, with stark
white interior and an
international menu of
dishes inspired by the
cuisines of Italy, Thailand,
Japan and New Zealand,
among others. Baked

langoustine, ostrich and
lamb are some of the
options.
☎ 222 326 203 ✉ Pařížská
třída 17 ☽ noon-midnight
Ⓜ Staroměstská

Ristorante Isabella
(4, D2)
Italian/seafood €€€€
In the brick-vaulted cellar
of the Bellagio Hotel (p98),
Isabella is a highly rated
Italian restaurant, presided
over by 'celebrity' Swedish
chef Lars Sjö.strand. Seafood
dishes such as shellfish
panna cotta and seared
blue-fin tuna dominate
the menu, alongside pasta
and risotto.
☎ 224 819 957 ✉ U
milosrydných 2 ☽ 6-11pm
Ⓜ Staroměstská

U Krkavců (4, E2)
Modern Czech €€€-€€€€
For something more ex-
otic, try this underground
vault. Peach stuffed with
lobster mayonnaise makes
an unusual starter, while
main dishes include a lamb
stroganoff and swordfish in
caviar sauce.
☎ 224 817 264 ✉ Dlouhá
25 ☽ noon-3pm &

6pm-midnight Apr-Oct,
6pm-midnight Nov-Mar
Ⓜ Náměstí Republiky

MALÁ STRANA

Cantina (5, C5)
Mexican €
Convivial Latin eatery,
just opposite the Petřín Hill
tramway, where you can
dine under a ceiling of
coffee-sacks on the usual
array of chilli con carne,
enchiladas and quesadillas.
There's also a well-stocked
cocktail bar.
☎ 257 317 173 ✉ Újezd 38
☽ noon-midnight Ⓜ Ma-
lostranská, then take tram
12, 22 or 57 to Újezd ♿ Ⓥ

Černý Orel (5, C3)
Italian €€
The 'Black Eagle' is a
smart Italian restaurant
with a Czech twist, serving
all the expected spaghetti,
tagliatelle and bruscetta,
plus the odd Czech intruder
such as goulash and a
few grilled fish and roast
meat dishes.
☎ 257 533 207 ✉ Malos-
transké náměstí 14 (entrance
on Zámecká) ☽ 11am-11pm
Ⓜ Malostranská ♿ Ⓥ

WAITER, THERE'S A VIEW IN MY SOUP
For great river views, try tucking into fresh fish at
C'est La Vie (p70), or perhaps dine on the terraces
of **Hergetova Cihelna** (p70) or **Střelecký Ostrov
Restaurant** (p71).
   Hanavský pavilón (4, B1; ☎ 233 323 641; Letenské
sady 173) is an elaborate 1891 pavilion with good seafood, game and breathtaking views. **U Zlaté studně**
(5, C2; ☎ 257 533 322; U Zlaté Studně 4), in the hotel
of the same name, has a fantastic vista. Highest of
them all is the **Tower Restaurant** (6, E4; ☎ 242 418
778; Mahlerovy sady 1) in Žižkov's TV Tower (p32).

TEA TIME IN PRAGUE

Since the mid-1990s, a number of smokeless, tranquil tearooms (*čajovny*) have won popularity in Prague.

One of the most attractive spots for a pot of oolong is **Guan Yin Čajovna** (6, C4; ☎ 224 910 816; Náplavni 7; ⏱ 10am-9pm Mon-Fri, noon-9pm Sat & Sun), where you can lounge on cushions on the floor amid Chinese lacquerware.

U Božího Mlýna (3, A2-A3; ☎ 222 519 128; Lublaňská 50) is a subterranean chill-out spot with a big list of teas and health drinks. **Pod stromen čajovým** (3, C1; ☎ 222 251 045; Mánesova 55) serves 130 blends of tea, as well as Czech mead.

U zeleného čaje (5, B3; ☎ 257 530 027; Nerudova 19) offers such tea-based concoctions as 'boiling communist', 'grandmother's caress' and 'soaking dog'. Meanwhile, **Čajovna Siva** (7, D1; ☎ 222 315 983; Masná 8; ⏱ noon-midnight) has a touch of the souk about it, with hookah-pipes at hand if you fancy a puff on some exotically flavoured tobacco.

C'est La Vie (4, A5)

French/seafood €€€€
Crisp white linen tablecloths, candles and mellow music make for a civilised dining experience at C'est La Vie. Sit down to delectable dishes such as trout in champagne sauce, grilled monkfish and Atlantic scallops. There's a riverside terrace if you prefer to dine alfresco, and live jazz on weekend afternoons.
☎ 257 321 511 ✉ Říční 1
⏱ 11.30am-1am
Ⓜ Národní Třída, then tram 6, 9, 22 or 58 to Vítězná ♿

David (5, B3)

Modern Czech €€-€€€
Hidden away on a side lane, David's specialises in game such as guinea fowl, partridge and quail. There are also a few fishy options – try the marinated salmon with caviar. Abstract art by Prague painter Míchel Halva is on sale here too.
☎ 257 533 109 ✉ Tržiště 21 ⏱ 11.30am-11pm
Ⓜ Malostranská

El Centro (5, C4)

Spanish €-€€
Tapas, paella and lots of Spanish-style seafood dishes are served at this rustic little 'bodega'. Alternatives include lamb and pork, and there's a good choice of wines.
☎ 257 533 343
✉ Maltézské náměstí 9
⏱ noon-midnight
Ⓜ Malostranská

Hergetova Cihelna (4, B3)

International €€€-€€€€
Trendy bar, restaurant and cocktail lounge with a great view of Charles Bridge from its riverside terrace. Try such diverse dishes as yellow-fin tuna sashimi, porcine risotto and poached lemon sole.

Sip an aperitif at, allegedly, Prague's longest bar.
☎ 257 535 534 ⌨ www .cihelna.com ✉ Cihelná 2b ⏱ 10am-1am Ⓜ Malostranská Ⓥ

Kampa Park (4, A3)

Modern Czech/seafood €€€€
Exclusive restaurant/bar complex claiming the northern end of Kampa, giving its clientele magical views of the river, particularly at night. Serves top-class international food and wine to famous types, who then get listed on the back of a brochure.
☎ 257 532 685 ✉ Na Kampě 8b ⏱ 11.30am-late Ⓜ Malostranská Ⓥ

Restaurant Alchymist (4, A4)

Modern Czech/Italian €€€-€€€€
With all its zebra-print, golden chairs, heavy red

drapes and sparkling crystal chandeliers, the restaurant of the Residence Nosticova (p99) looks like it's throwing a party for Elton John. Slip on your shades and try some fine cuisine such as tandoori rack of lamb, or linguini with mussels.

☎ 257 312 518 ▢ www .alchymist.cz ✉ Hellichova 4 🕘 noon-3pm & 7-11pm Ⓜ Malostranská, then tram 12, 22 or 23 to Hellichova

Square (5, C3)

Mediterranean €€€-€€€€

The trendy Square specialises in tapas, pasta and seafood, clam risotto, roast squid with saffron and duck prosciutto. English breakfasts are served until 4pm.

☎ 296 826 114 ▢ www .squarerestaurant.cz ✉ Malostanské náměstí 5 🕘 9am-1am Sun-Wed, 9am-3am Thu-Sat Ⓜ Malostranská

Střelecký Ostrov Restaurant (4, B6)

Modern Czech €€-€€€€

This modish restaurant on 'Marksmen's Island' offers fine cuisine such as guinea fowl with shiitake mushrooms and salmon in cognac sauce. Great river views, salads and pizzas can be had on the outdoor terrace upstairs.

☎ 224 934 026 ▢ www.streleckyostrov.cz ✉ Střelecký Ostrov 336 🕘 noon-midnight Ⓜ Národní Třída, then tram No 6, 9, 22 or 23 to most Legií

U Maltézských rytířů (5, C4)

Traditional Czech €€

This cosy olde-worlde restaurant has an extensive wine list, while good-value meals include hearty dishes such as saddle of boar in briar sauce, and grilled pike.

☎ 257 530 075 ▢ www .umaltezskychrytiru.cz ✉ Prokopská 10 🕘 11am-11pm Ⓜ Malostranská ♿

U Tří Zlatých Hvězd (5, C3)

Traditional Czech €-€€

The mystical murals make this place look like an alchemist's antechamber, and the usual Bohemian specialities are on offer, including onion soup, pork and dumplings, and roast meats. The set menus (from around 180Kč) are very good value.

☎ 257 531 636 ✉ Malostranské náměstí 8 🕘 11.30am-11.30pm Ⓜ Malostranská

NOVÉ MĚSTO

Albio (4, G2)

Vegetarian/health €

A fresh-looking 'wholefood' restaurant, Albio is decked out in lots of pine and ropes. This health food heaven sources all its food from local organic farms, and has its own onsite bakery. The tempting dishes include rye gnocchi, whole-wheat pasta and salads, and there are plenty of organic wines and health drinks to go with it.

☎ 222 317 902 ▢ www .albiostyl.cz ✉ Truhlářská 18 🕘 11.30am-10pm Mon-Fri Ⓜ Náměstí Republiky ♿ Ⓥ

Bohemia Bagel Express (3, A2)

Takeaway café/breakfast €

This tiny kiosk – the smallest of Prague's three-branch bagel chain sells great excellent-value filled bagels, muffins, salads and coffee, including various cheap 'meal deals'. There are a couple of tables to lean on outside.

☎ 603 196 636 ✉ Tylovo náměstí 🕘 7.30am-6.30pm Ⓜ IP Pavlova Ⓥ

Ultramodern Cafe Screen (p72) in Hotel Imperial

Box Block (4, H3)
Italian/fusion €€€€

An elegant theatre for fine dining, the restaurant of the luxurious Carlo IV hotel (p99) has marble floors and frescoes . The menu offers such treats as turbot in truffle sauce, bison steak with prosciutto San Daniele, and tuna carpaccio with Chardonnay jelly.
☎ 224 593 040
✉ Senovážné náměstí 13
⏱ 11.30am-3pm & 6-11pm
Ⓜ Hlavní Nádraží

Café Screen (4, G2)
Café €

Futuristic-looking café (Jetsons style), with its primary colours, translucent plastic seating and TV screens continually playing MTV. Pizzas, baguettes, salads and delicious stuffed savoury pancakes compose the menu, and there's free Internet access for customers.
☎ 224 816 607 ✉ Na Poříčí 15 ⏱ 9am-midnight
Ⓜ Náměstí Republiky Ⓥ

Cafe Slavia (4, C5)
Café €-€€

A once-famous literary café, where performers and patrons of the National Theatre would gather to chat over coffee. It's a classy place with great views over the river, though the salads and chicken and chips-style dishes are uninspiring. Sit back with a *seksint* (the house cocktail of Bohemian champagne and absinthe) and enjoy the atmosphere.
☎ 224 239 604 ✉ Národní třída 1 ⏱ 8am-11pm
Ⓜ Národní Třída 🚻 Ⓥ

Café Tramvaj (4, F5)
Café €

All aboard for lunch! Sandwiches, salads and pizzas are served up at this pair of vintage tramcars parked in the middle of Wenceslas Square, and while the food might be unexceptional, the novelty value will entrance younger kids.
☎ 724 072 753 ✉ Václavské náměstí 32 ⏱ 9am-midnight Mon-Sat, 10am-midnight Sun Ⓜ Můstek
🚻 Ⓥ

Don Pedro (6, C4)
Colombian €€-€€€

The Czech Republic's only Colombian restaurant is a friendly, brightly decorated place where you can try such exotica as plantains and yucca. The Colombian dishes are a touch beef-heavy, but burritos, enchiladas and other Mexican fare are available too, and the drinks are great.
☎ 224 923 505 ✉ Masarykovo Nábřeží 2
⏱ 11.20am-11.30pm
Ⓜ Karlovo Náměstí Ⓥ

East-West (4, F5)
International €€

Billed as a 'Native' restaurant, this little place, just inside the Lucerna Passage, serves some unusual options such as Tibetan chicken curry, nasi goreng and mussels in white-wine sauce, as well as simple baked potato dishes.
☎ 296 236 513
✉ Štěpánská 61 ⏱ 8am-midnight Ⓜ Můstek Ⓥ

Green Tomato (4, G4)
Pizzeria €€

This place has gone for the Art Nouveau–salon effect. There's lots of mirrors, fancy lampshades and gilt-framed paintings,successfully making an unusually pleasant setting for an inexpensive pizza-and-pasta parlour.

Cafe Slavia was once a hotbed for Prague's literati

CORPORATE CUISINE

There are plenty of perfect places for formal meals, deal-making or just plain entertaining. **Restaurant Flambée** (7, B3-B4; ☎ 224 248 512; Husova 5) is an exclusive cellar retreat, patronised by diplomats and Hollywood stars. Inside the Hilton Hotel is **Café Bistro** (4, J1; ☎ 224 842 727; Pobřežní 1), a good 24-hour place to casually impress a business connection. **La Perle de Prague** (below) is the ultimate in fashionable fine dining, and **La Scène** (p68) has top-quality French cuisine and a trendy champagne bar.

☎ 224 232 271 ⊠ Jindřišská 18 🕓 10am-11pm Mon-Sat, noon-10pm Sun 🅜 Náměstí Republiky 🖫 🔽

Highland Restaurant (6, C5)
Steakhouse €€
Carnivores – Caledonian or otherwise – will enjoy this place, serving up hefty portions of Scottish highland steaks in various forms. It also has ostrich, kangaroo and pasta.
☎ 224 922 511 ⊠ Gorazdova 22 🕓 10am-11.30pm Mon-Fri, noon-11.30pm Sat & Sun 🅜 Karlovo Náměstí

Hot (4, F5)
Asian/fusion €€€-€€€€
Flashy and fashionable, Hot is a self-consciously stylish place with plush seating, overlooking Wenceslas Square. It serves a mixture of Asian and Pacific dishes, including lots of fish. Oysters, tiger prawns and monkfish sashimi are some of the possibilities.
☎ 222 247 240 ⊠ Václavské náměstí 45 🕓 8.30am-1am 🅜 Muzeum

Kavárna Imperial (4, G2)
Café €
Splendid *belle époque* coffee house, lavishly decorated with yellow-and-cream ceramic tiling and mosaics throughout. Unremarkable Chinese dishes, omelettes and steaks feature on the menu. Stick to the coffee and cake, and beware the flying doughnuts. Live jazz/Dixieland bands Friday and Saturday evenings.
☎ 602 368 702 ⊠ Na Poříčí 15 🕓 9am-11pm 🅜 Náměstí Republiky 🖫 🔽

La Perle de Prague (6, C5)
French/seafood €€€€
Atop the Dancing Building (p30), this formal restaurant has panoramic views and some of the best seafood in the city, including poached turbot with seaweed cream, scallops in saffron sauce, and lobster, as well as duck dishes. There are also some excellent wines, and the service is faultless. The two-course 'business lunch' (490Kč, Monday to Friday) is great value.
☎ 221 984 160 ⊠ 7th floor, Dancing Building, Rašínovo nábřeží 80

🕓 7-10.30pm Mon, noon-2pm & 7-10.30pm Tue-Sat 🅜 Karlovo Náměstí

Lemon Leaf (6, C5)
Thai €-€€
The bright, spacious and plant-filled interior of this popular Thai place is immediately inviting. Traditional Thai curries and noodles share the menu with intriguing dishes such as grilled plaice marinated in seaweed.
☎ 224 919 056 🖳 www.lemon.cz ⊠ Na Zderaze 14 🕓 11am-11pm Mon-Thu, 11am-12.30am Fri, 12.30pm-midnight Sat, 12.30-11pm Sun 🅜 Karlovo Náměstí 🔽

Peking (6, D5)
Chinese €€-€€€
Right outside IP Pavlova metro station, colourful Peking is one of Prague's better Chinese restaurants, specialising in seafood, dim sum and Peking duck. It also has a takeaway service.
☎ 222 520 888 ⊠ Legerova 64 🕓 11am-11pm 🅜 IP Pavlova 🔽

Picante (4, F2)
Mexican/takeaway café €
Busy takeaway serving a vast range of nachos, tacos and other hot Mexican fast food at very reasonable prices. There are plenty of vegetarian options.
☎ 222 322 022 ⊠ Revoluční 4 🕓 24hr 🅜 Náměstí Republiky

Restaurace MD Rettigové (4, F2)
Traditional Czech €€
This restaurant boldly claims to be the only restaurant in Bohemia named after Magdaleny Dobromily

Lavishly decorated Kàvarna Imperial (p73)

Rettigové, an 18th-century Czech cook-book author. Local favourites such as baked duck, pike and trout are available, plus oddities such as 'Count Elmer's tongue' (beef tongue with sprouts). Mmmm!
☎ 222 314 483
✉ Truhlářská 4 ⊙ 11am-11pm Ⓜ Náměstí Republiky

Restaurace Podskalská Celnice Na Výtoni (6, C5)
Traditional Czech/pub grub €-€€
On the ground floor of the 16th-century Podskalí Customs House, traditional venison, pork, duck and fish dishes are served. The tables outside provide a pleasant setting for a few quiet beers away from the nearby above. Upstairs, there's a little museum (see p27).

☎ 224 921 933 ✉ Rašín-ovo nábřeží 412 ⊙ 10am-11pm Ⓣ 3, 7, 16 or 17

Taj Mahal (4, G6)
Indian €€-€€€
Hidden behind the National Museum, this brightly decorated Indian restaurant serves all the usual suspects: chicken tikka masala, kormas and vindaloos with Western tastes in mind. Live music most evenings.
☎ 224 225 566 ✉ Škretova 10 ⊙ 11.30am-11.30pm Mon-Fri, 1-11pm Sat & Sun Ⓜ Muzeum Ⓥ

U Rozvařilů (4, G2)
Café €
Old-style cafeteria with a slightly institutional feel, but unbeatable for cheap meals and cheap beer. Unless you speak Czech, however, you'll have to point at what

takes your fancy and trust to luck. There's a restaurant with a bigger menu at the back.
✉ Na Poříčí 26 ⊙ cafeteria 8am-8pm Mon-Fri, 9am-7pm Sat, 10am-6pm Sun; restaurant 2-7pm Mon-Fri
Ⓜ Náměstí Republiky Ⓥ

Žofín (4, B6)
Modern Czech €€€€
This neo-Renaissance palace was built on an island in the Vltava during the 19th century, and is now a stunning gourmet restaurant. Dine on lobsters beneath the chandeliers, or the separate garden restaurant, with children's play area, provides cheap and filling fare.
☎ 224 919 139 ✉ Slovan-ský ostrov ⊙ 11am-midnight Ⓜ Karlovo Náměstí Ⓖ Ⓥ

STARÉ MĚSTO

Ambiente Restaurante Brasileiro (7, F2)
Brazilian €€€
This busy slice of Brazil offers two all-you-can-eat menus; the 'churrasco' menu (525Kč), with continually circulating waiters carving off slices of freshly prepared meat onto your plate, or the lighter buffet (245Kč), with sushi, salads, oysters, soup, fish and much more. Reservations are advisable.
☎ 221 451 200 ✉ Slovan-ský Dům, Na Příkopě 22 ⊙ noon-midnight
Ⓜ Náměstí Republiky

Ambiente Ristorante Pasta Fresca (7, D2)
Italian €€€
Another branch of the glossy Ambiente chain, this hugely

popular place is a good choice for quality pasta and fish dishes. Service is speedy and the wine is good too. Again, book ahead for dinner. ☎ 224 230 244 ⊠ Celetná 11 ⏱ 11am-midnight Ⓜ Náměstí Republiky Ⓥ

Beas (7, D1)
Vegetarian €
Small vegetarian café hidden away in a little courtyard off Týnská. There's a simple menu of the lentil-soup-and-salad variety, and some outdoor seating.
☎ 777 165 478 ⊠ Týnská 19 ⏱ 8.30am-8pm Mon-Fri, 10am-6pm Sat & Sun Ⓜ Náměstí Republiky Ⓖ Ⓥ

Bohemia Bagel (7, D1)
Takeaway café/breakfast €
Inexpensive filled bagels, sandwiches, salads and English- and American-style breakfasts are the orders of the day at this casual backpacker hang-out. There's also Internet access and a kids' play area. It can get rather smoky and noisy at times, though. There is also another branch on Újezd (5, C6).

☎ 224 812 560 ⊒ www.bo hemiabagel.cz ⊠ Masná 2 ⏱ 7am-midnight Mon-Fri, 8am-midnight Sat & Sun Ⓜ Náměstí Republiky Ⓖ Ⓥ

Country Life (7, C3)
Vegetarian €
Busy buffet-style vegetarian food hall connected to the health food shop of the same name, with a menu of hot meals and salads. The ultrahealthy unprocessed, unrefined, nondairy food is charged according to weight. Strictly no smoking. ☎ 224 213 373 ⊠ Melant-richova 15 ⏱ 9am-8pm Mon-Thu, 9am-6pm Fri, 11am-8pm Sun Ⓜ Můstek Ⓖ Ⓥ

Culinaria (4, D4)
Takeaway/café €
Attractive deli offers freshly made sandwiches, a variety of salads and scrumptious cakes. Culinaria also has a juice bar and light meals to eat in or take away. Homesick visitors with too much spare change can also pick up essential imported oddments such as Marmite,

Wholesome Country Life

shortbread, HP Sauce and mustard powder.
☎ 224 247 237 ⊒ www .culinaria.cz ⊠ Skořepka 9 ⏱ 8.30am-8pm Mon-Fri, 10am-7pm Sat, noon-5pm Sun Ⓜ Můstek Ⓥ

Ebel Coffee House (7, B3)
Café/breakfast €
One of several branches of the popular coffee house, this is a quiet spot for coffee, tea and cakes, or a glass or two of wine. Breakfast, muffins, sandwiches and salads are

GOING GREEN
Vegetarian food in Prague ranges from pure, expertly prepared cuisine (Albio; p71) to cheap, wholesome buffet fare (Country Life; above) and ethnic variations (Beas; above), as well as some pretty poor imitations. Dedicated vegetarian restaurants are quite rare in the inner city.

Be wary of places that appear in generic 'Vegetarian' listings in tourist leaflets; quite often they exaggerate to get the trade. Except in authentic vegetarian places, check the ingredients in the dishes, as it's not uncommon for your potential veggie meal to include fish or even pork.

also served. There's another outlet in Týnský dvůr.
☎ 222 222 018
✉ Řetězová 9 ⏰ 8am-8pm
Ⓜ Staroměstská

Francouzská (7, F2)
French €€€€
The grand main restaurant of the even grander Municipal House (p15) is a haven for fine dining. *Coq au vin, bouillabaisse* and swordfish are some of the gourmet offerings, or you could opt for the cheaper three-course 'quick lunch' menu (490Kč), which changes regularly.
☎ 222 002 770 ✉ Municipal House, Náměstí Republiky 5 ⏰ noon-4pm & 6-11pm Mon-Sat, 11.30am-3pm & 6-11pm Sun
Ⓜ Náměstí Republiky ♿

Grand Café Orient (7, E2)
Café €
The only cubist café in the world opened in the House of the Black Madonna in 1912. It closed in the 1920s, but this exact reproduction opened in 2005. Stripy seats, angular furnishings and a pianist tinkling in the corner make an atmospheric spot for cocktails, sandwiches and salads.
☎ 224 224 240 ✉ Ovocný trh 19 ⏰ 9am-10pm
Ⓜ Náměstí Republiky Ⓥ

Jáchymka (7,C1)
Traditional Czech/beer hall €
A reasonable selection of Czech standards, of the pork-and-dumplings variety, is on offer here, as well as several different beers to wash it all down in good old Prague fashion.
☎ 224 819 621 ✉ Jáchýmova 4 ⏰ 10am-11pm
Ⓜ Staroměstská ♿

Kavárna obecní dům (7, F2)
Café €-€€
Chandelier-lit café in the Art Nouveau Municipal House (p15). Salads and sandwiches are staples, or you could plump for the three-course 'tourist menu' (250Kč). The groaning dessert trolley is continually wheeled around to tempt you further, while live jazz bands tootle away in the corner.
☎ 222 002 763 ✉ Municipal House, Náměstí Republiky 5 ⏰ 7.30am-11pm
Ⓜ Náměstí Republiky ♿ Ⓥ

Klub Architektů (4, D4)
Modern Czech €€-€€€
Claustrophobics and nyctophobics might not enjoy this cramped, candle-lit cellar restaurant (and it does get stuffy), but the inventive modern cuisine is excellent, with fascinating dishes such as lamb with juniper berries, figs and 'old Czech-style gingerbread spices'.
☎ 224 401 214 ✉ Betlémské náměstí 5A ⏰ 11.30am-midnight Ⓜ Národní Třída

Le Terroir (4, D4)
French €€€
Classic French cuisine involving langoustines, fresh fish, rabbit and lamb is served at this atmospheric restaurant set in a 12th-century building known as 'At the Old Ball House'. You can sample some of the 600-plus wines on offer in the Romanesque cellars, and buy wine and cheese to take away.
☎ 602 889 118 🖳 www.leterroir.cz ✉ Vejvodova 1 (entrance on Jilská)
⏰ 11am-11pm Ⓜ Můstek

Made in Japan (4, D4)
Japanese €€
If you're in the mood for raw fish, then this smart sushi bar

Alfresco dining at Municipal House's Kavárna obecní dům

Keep cool at Klub Architektů

may be what you're looking for. Tempura, noodles, salads, soups and fish steaks are also available.
☎ 224 235 604 ⌨ www .madeinjapan.cz ✉ Rytířská 10 🕙 11am-midnight M Můstek Ⓥ

Millhouse Sushi (7, F2)
Japanese €-€€€
Tired of shopping? Sit up to the conveyor belt and help yourself to nigiri, maki sushi, sashimi, tempura and other Japanese mouthfuls in the courtyard of the Slovanský Dům shopping mall. Colour-coded dishes cost between 60Kč and 280Kč, or for 680Kč you can eat all you want for two hours. No credit cards.
☎ 221 451 771 ⌨ www .millhouse-sushi.cz ✉ Slovanský Dům, Na Příkopě 22 🕙 11am-11pm M Náměstí Republiky Ⓥ

Pizzeria Rusantino (7, D1)
Pizzeria €
Cheap, friendly, brightly painted pizza place serving up all the usual budget Italian fare, including lots of pasta and gnocchi dishes, and the odd salad or two.

☎ 222 318 172 ✉ Dušní 4 🕙 11am-11pm M Staroměstská Ⓥ

Plzeňská (7, F2)
Traditional Czech €€
In the basement of Municipal House (p15), this Art Nouveau hall is all stained glass, chandeliers and polished wood. Meat-heavy specialities such as pork, pike, lamb stroganoff, and Prague ham and gherkins dominate, though the odd vegetarian choice inadvertently slips through.
☎ 222 002 780 ✉ Náměstí Republiky 5 🕙 11.30am-11pm M Náměstí Republiky 🚹 Ⓥ

Rasoi (4, E2)
Indian €€€
Everything from the chef down to the cutlery comes straight from India, so this is as authentic as you're going to get in Prague. All the popular tandoori, jalfrezi and biryani dishes are there, and are done well, though the atmosphere is a little subdued.
☎ 222 328 400 ⌨ www .rasoi.cz ✉ Dlouhá 13 🕙 noon-11.30pm M Náměstí Republiky 🚹 Ⓥ

Reykjavík (7, A3)
Seafood/Scandinavian €€€-€€€€
Owned by Iceland's honorary consul-general in Prague, Reykjavík serves Nordic staples such as salted herrings, eel and, perhaps more palatably, salmon and chips. The menu gives insightful titbits, such as the fact that 60% of Icelanders allegedly believe in elves, but service is slow and jaded.
☎ 222 221 218 ⌨ www .reykjavik.cz ✉ Karlova 20 🕙 11am-midnight M Staroměstská

If you knew Sushi...

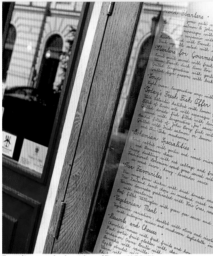
Tantalise tastebuds with truffles at V Zátiší

Rybí trh (7, E1)
Seafood €€€€
One of Prague's finest seafood restaurants, 'Fish Market' lives up to its name by acquiring fresh catches daily (see the mound of ice inside) and preparing it as you wish. Specialities include *bouillabaisse*, caviar and fresh lobster plucked from the internal aquarium.
☎ 224 895 447 ✉ Týnský dvůr 5 ⏰ 11am-midnight Ⓜ Náměstí Republiky

Sarah Bernhardt (7, F2)
French/modern Czech €€€€
Dine in style in the exquisite Art Nouveau restaurant of the Hotel Paříž (p98), where luxurious possibilities include flambéed scallops and butterfish with truffles. Sunday brunch (from noon to 4pm) is extremely popular, and features live music.
☎ 222 195 195 ✉ Hotel Paříž, U Obecního domu 1

⏰ noon-4pm & 6pm-midnight Ⓜ Náměstí Republiky

Tequila Sunrise (7, D2-E2)
Mexican €
Though aimed principally at the passing tourists (viz the sombreros and Spanish dolls), Tequila Sunrise still turns out reasonable tacos, fajitas, burritos and so on. There's also a convivial little bar at the front.
☎ 224 819 383
✉ Štupartská 6 ⏰ 11am-11pm Ⓜ Náměstí Republiky

Týnská Literary Cafe (7, D2)
Café €
Slightly pretentious publisher-run café patronised by moody literary types, who want to be seen being moody. There's a peaceful courtyard where you can rub your chin while reading Kierkegaard, or just chat over coffee.
☎ 224 827 807 🖥 www.knihytynska.cz ✉ Týnská 6

⏰ 9am-11pm Mon-Fri, 10am-11pm Sat & Sun Ⓜ Náměstí Republiky

V Zátiší (4, C4)
Modern Czech €€€-€€€€
This gourmet place serves excellent Czech and international cuisine. Try asparagus with truffle and Tokay wine dressing, grilled langoustines or roast rabbit. The two/three-course lunch menu (weekdays only), including a drink, is reasonable value at 695/795Kč.
☎ 222 221 155 ✉ Liliová 1 ⏰ noon-3pm & 5.30-11pm Ⓜ Můstek

VINOHRADY

Amigos (3, B1)
Tex-Mex €€
Amigos is a busy, sombrero-bedecked haven for tacos, nachos, chimichangas and quesadillas, and plenty of veggie options. Steaks and seafood are also available. The 69Kč weekday lunch special is a bargain. The tables are packed in rather tightly though.
☎ 222 250 594 🖥 www.amigos.cz ✉ Anny Letenské 16 ⏰ 11.30am-midnight Ⓜ Náměstí Míru
♿ Ⓥ

Bumerang (3, A2)
Australian €-€€
Cellar restaurant and bar appealing to homesick antipodeans with didgeridoos hanging from the walls and Australian wines and beers behind the bar. Soups, steaks and grills are served, and two-course set lunches, with beer, go for between 64Kč and 89Kč, changing daily.

☎ 222 517 047 ▯ www
.52.cz ✉ Londýnská 52
🕙 11am-midnight Mon-Fri,
5pm-midnight Sat & Sun
Ⓜ Náměstí Míru

Cheers (3, B2)
International €-€€
This bright and smiley bar-
restaurant serves an eclectic
range of dishes from around
the world, with Thai, Greek,
Italian, Japanese and Mexican cuisine represented. Try
the tofu salad, kebabs, fish
and chips, duck or pasta with
blue cheese sauce. There's an
equally long list of drinks.
☎ 222 513 108 ▯ www
.cheers.cz ✉ Belgicka 116
🕙 11am-1am Ⓜ Náměstí
Míru Ⓥ

Los v Oslu (6, E4)
Scandinavian €€
The 'Moose in Oslo' is an
unexpected find on this
quiet side street. The food is
excellent, and includes dishes
such as Norwegian seafood
goulash, shark fillet, 'caramel
flavoured chicken' and lots
of beef. Try the indulgent
Finnish cheesecake.
☎ 222 513 295 ✉ Peru-
nova 17 🕙 noon-1am
Mon-Fri, 1pm-1am Sat,
1pm-midnight Sun
Ⓜ Jiřího z Poděbrad

Mehana Sofia (3, B3)
Bulgarian €-€€
Downstairs in the Hotel
Sofia, this is an authentic
slice of the Balkans, down
to the boarskins on the wall.
Sample traditional Bulgarian
dishes such as *kebapcheta*
(grilled sausages) and *kyufte*
(meatballs) or, if you're feeling brave, you might like the
buttered tripe...
☎ 603 298 865 ✉ Amer-
ická 28 🕙 noon-11pm
Ⓜ Náměstí Míru ♿ Ⓥ

Rudý Baron (3, C2)
Modern Czech €€
You're not likely to find too
many Red Baron–themed
restaurants around, so if you
have a hankering to dine out
beneath biplane propellers
and photos of WWI German
air-aces, then Rudý Baron is
for you. Meaty items on the
menu include roast piglet
and roast duck in honey
☎ 222 513 610 ✉ Korunní
23 🕙 11am-midnight Mon-
Fri, noon-midnight Sat & Sun
Ⓜ Náměstí Míru

Tiger Tiger (3, B1)
Thai €€
One of the best places in
the city for Thai cuisine.
Tiger Tiger's tasty specialities
include chicken coconut soup

and *pad thai* (fried noodles,
tofu, tamarind, onions
and egg), plus lots of traditional curries; to save face,
heat levels are indicated,
and there's a 100Kč
lunch menu.
☎ 222 512 084 ▯ www
.tigertiger.cz ✉ Anny Letenské 5 🕙 11.30am-11pm
Mon-Fri, 5-11pm Sat & Sun
Ⓜ Náměstí Míru Ⓥ

Ztráty & Nálezy (3, A1)
Traditional Czech/
pub grub €€
Duck, beef, pork, salmon
and vegetarian options are
offered at this amenable
pub-restaurant, along with
some more unusual modern
twists such as chicken with
raisins and pears. Vintage
sporting equipment, street
signs and an old bicycle
decorate the walls.
☎ 224 216 389 ✉ Vino-
hradská 14 🕙 11.30am-
11pm Ⓜ Náměstí Míru Ⓥ

WORTH A TRIP

Brasserie Ullman (6, C3)
Modern Czech €-€€
This terrace restaurant,
in the middle of Letná
Gardens, has a sophisticated
menu at reasonable prices.
Try monkfish wrapped in

STUFF TO SAVOUR
Try these places to pump up your sugar levels or to
take a break from the taste of goulash and dumplings.
Cream & Dream (7, B3; ☎ 224 211 035; Husova 12)
For lots of exotically swirled, fruity Italian ice cream.
Gourmand au Gourmand (7, D1; ☎ 222 329 060;
Dlouhá 10) Has luscious tarts, cakes and pastries, and
some of the best ice cream around.
Paneria (4, F2; ☎ 224 827 401; Dlouhá 25) Stocks
tarts, sandwiches, and filled croissants and baguettes.

Cream & Dream (p79), another phrase for ice-cream paradise

lime leaves. It's right behind the cheap beer garden.

☎ 233 378 200 ✉ Letná Gardens, Letná ⏲ noon-10pm Ⓜ Vltavská

Corso (6, D3)
Italian/traditional Czech €-€€
Though Corso has more ceiling decorations and painted glass than many churches, its menu is all straightforward pasta dishes and traditional Czech cooking. Corso also serves more than twenty different Czech wines if you fancy a tipple.

☎ 220 806 541 ✉ Dukelských Hrdinů 48, Holešovice ⏲ 9am-11pm Ⓜ Vltavská

Hombre del Mundo (6, B5)
Mexican €€
This smart pub-restaurant provides a relaxed ambience and snappy service in the smart part of Smíchov. Tacos,

burritos, enchiladas and the like can be had, along with fish and salads, and it's regularly full of local shoppers taking a break over a few beers.

☎ 257 326 902 🖳 www .hombredelmundo.cz ✉ Nádražní 21, Smíchov ⏲ 11am-midnight Ⓜ Anděl Ⓥ

Na Verandách (6, B5)
Pub grub €
Another big, brassy pub-restaurant in Smíchov, attached to the famous Staropramen brewery, so it's the perfect place to sample the full range of their output. Fish and chips, platters of sausages, pork joints and other fare designed to accompany your beer are served.

☎ 257 191 200 ✉ Nádražní 84, Smíchov ⏲ 11am-midnight Ⓜ Anděl

Ouky Douky (6, D3)
Café/breakfast €
With nine different set breakfasts (from 92Kč), plus lots of snacks, sandwiches and drinks, Ouky Douky makes a great pit-stop for those visiting the museums and galleries in Holešovice. Sit in the busy café or the adjoining second-hand bookshop. It also has Internet access (15Kč per 10 minutes).

☎ 266 711 531 🖳 www.oukydouky.cz ✉ Janovského 14, Holešovice ⏲ 8am-midnight Ⓜ Vltavská Ⓥ

Rezavá Kotva (6, C4)
Café €
Perched on the tip of Dětský ostrov, this place has some great views downriver. There's a small indoor bar and a breezy, open decking area where you can tuck into sandwiches, salads, baked potatoes and bigger meals such as grilled trout.

☎ 777 550 005 ✉ Dětský ostrov, Smíchov ⏲ 9am-2am Mon-Sat, noon-midnight Sun Ⓜ Anděl Ⓥ

U Vyšehradské Rotundy (6, C5)
Italian/traditional Czech €-€€
Inside the Vyšehrad castle compound, this quiet place has a small garden where you can enjoy beer and sausages and gaze at Prague's oldest Romanesque rotunda. There's a big list of pizzas, gnocchi and so on, plus steaks.

☎ 224 919 970 ✉ K rotundě 3, Vyšehrad ⏲ 11am-11pm Ⓜ Vyšehrad Ⓥ

Entertainment

Everywhere you look in this cosmopolitan city, there's something intriguing going on: superb classical music concerts in grand auditoria, cool jazz in chilled-out smoky cellars, ultramodern dance clubs, trendy cocktail bars and good old Prague pubs. If you're in the mood for something a little different, why not attend a black-light theatre: it's a kind of back-lit pantomime and makes for a novel experience. Puppetry shows continue to delight kids.

Many places cater exclusively for the tourists, and often charge accordingly. Numerous churches, for example, stage nightly music performances – you'll be handed flyers every five minutes in the Old Town – but these can sometimes be fairly lacklustre affairs. One much publicised feature of recent years has been the arrival of the largely British 'stag-party' crowd in search of cheap beer – and lots of it. Not the most attractive of sights, but on the upside, it's easy to avoid the city-centre bars they frequent, and while away an evening over a few beers in one of countless convivial Czech pubs, with no embarassing trouser-droppers in sight.

Staré Město is replete with bars theatres, and live music joints, with some of the flashier ones crowded around Pařížská and in the maze of streets behind Týn Church – many good jazz spots lie between Old Town Square and Národní. Clubs are strewn from Smíchov to Holešovice and everywhere in-between, including the busy Malostranské náměstí. Hard-edged Žižkov is home to some arty cinemas, experimental performance venues, and gay clubs, which are also scattered around Vinohrady and the New Town. The area south of the National

Theatre to Myslíková is one of the freshest, hippest zones, with a lot of young clubs, bars and cafés.

Many publications have details of what's on, where, and if it's worth the bother. The Night & Day section of the weekly *Prague Post* covers everything. *Prague Monthly Guide* is a brief source of listings, while *Welcome to Prague* (45Kč) is a seasonal programme of cultural events. *Heart of Europe* is a free glossy monthly with details of galleries, theatres, clubs and music. *Houser* and *NVG Weekly* are both free weekly Czech-language booklets detailing clubs, cinemas and theatre. *Amigo* magazine covers the gay scene.

SPECIAL EVENTS

January
Febiofest (25–31 January) International Festival of Film, TV & Video prompts screenings of new international films across the Czech Republic.

March
AghaRTA Prague Jazz Festival (until December) Top-drawer jazz artists and orchestras play at AghaRTA and elsewhere in the city.

April
Musica Ecumenica (7–16 April) International Festival of Spiritual Music, in various ethereal venues around town.

Burning of the Witches (Pálení čarodějnic; 30 April) Not literally, just the traditional burning of brooms to ward off evil, accompanied by lots of backyard end-of-winter bonfires.

Musica Sacra Praga (Easter, August, October) The Festival of Sacred Music takes place in a number of churches and concert halls, presenting material by Brahms, Puccini and Dvořák among others.

May
Majáles (1 May) Student-celebrated spring festival with a parade from Jana Palacha to Old Town Square.

Festival of Chamber Music (3 May–3 June) Tribute to Czech composers and Mozart at Bertramka, site of a Mozart Museum in Smíchov

Prague Spring (Pražské jaro; 12 May–4 June) International Music Festival, the most prestigious classical music event in Prague held at various concert halls, churches and theatres.

June
ET Jam Rock and alternative music gig at Autokemp Džbán camping ground in Vokovice.

Dance Prague (Tanec Praha; 9–28 June) International Festival of Modern Dance, with innovative performances at various venues.

Ethnic Festival (17 June–23 September) Folklore performed at the Municipal Library theatre by traditionally costumed Czech and Slovakian ensembles.

July
Prague Proms (late July–early August) International festival of classical music at the Rudolfinum and Municipal House.

Prague Music Festival (22 July–13 August) Yet more classical concerts, shared between the Rudolfinum and Týn Church.

August
Verdi Festival (to September) Nothing but Verdi operas at the Prague State Opera.

September
Burčak Sweet, cider-like liquid syphoned off at the initial stage of fermentation of new grape crops, and available for only a few weeks every year.

Mozart Iuventus (4–29 September) Mozart Festival at Bertramka featuring young artists playing his tunes, plus compositions written for the occasion.

Prague Autumn (11 September–1 October) Same concept as the more esteemed Prague Spring International Music Festival, but in autumn. Held at the Rudolfinum and State Opera.

Svatováclavské slavnosti (16–28 September) St Wenceslas Festival of spiritual art, encompassing music, painting and sculpture.

October
International Jazz Festival (24-27 October) Traditional jazz at popular haunts such as Lucerna Music Bar and Reduta.

November
Musica Iudaica Festival of Jewish Music, focusing on the composers of Terezín.

December
Festival Bohuslava Martinů (Bohuslav Martinů Music Festival; 7–13 December) Classical music festival dedicated to a famous Czech composer of the 20th century.

BARS & PUBS

Alcohol Bar (7, C1)
The staggering selection of booze at this aptly named drinker's shrine includes 250 types of whisky and scarce gins and rums. It's spacious, so you don't have to worry about tottering into fellow connoisseurs, and has a well-stocked humidor. Gets going late.
☎ 224 811 744 🖳 www .alcoholbar.cz ✉ Dušní 6, Staré Město ⏰ 7pm-2am Ⓜ Staroměstská

Aloha Wave Lounge (4, D2)
It's Tiki time in Prague! Don your Hawaiian shirt and hang loose with a Mai Tai in this laid-back, retro cocktail lounge. Regular DJs and surf party sounds into the small hours.
☎ 724 055 704 🖳 www .alohapraha.cz ✉ Dušní 11, Josefov ⏰ café 8.30am-2am Sun-Tue, 8.30am-4am Wed-Sat; bar 6pm-2am Sun-Tue, 6pm-4am Wed-Sat Ⓜ Staroměstská

Bar & Books (7, D1)
This swanky new branch of the New York–based cocktail lounge is the kind of place F Scott Fitzgerald might have got soused in. If the lights are up, you can leaf through a few books while sipping your martini; ladies receive free cigars on Mondays.
☎ 224 808 250 🖳 www .barandbooks.net ✉ Týnská 19, Staré Město ⏰ 5pm-3am Ⓜ Staromětská

Bar Tato Kojkej (4, A5)
This picturesque little bar-cum-art gallery sits in an old mill in Kampa Park,

and it still has a working waterwheel, turning lazily away as the stream bubbles past. It's an agreeable spot to idle away an afternoon over a few cold beers.
☎ 257 323 102 🖳 www .tatokojkej.cz ✉ Kampa Park, Malá Strana ⏰ 10am-midnight 🚋 12, 20, 22 or 23

Bloody Freddy Bar (4, D4)
Bloody dark bar that's hidden away on a side street off Michalská, and popular with local youth and backpackers alike. There's a long menu of powerful cocktails and a selection of salads and sandwiches to munch while watching whatever's on the Eurosport channel.
✉ Vejvodova 6, Staré Město ⏰ 4pm-2am Ⓜ Můstek

Blue Light (5, C3)
Suitably dingy and atmospheric jazz cavern, where you can enjoy a relaxed drink and cast an eye over the vintage posters and records that deck the walls. Unfortunately, the jazz itself comes in recorded rather than live form.

☎ 257 533 126 ✉ Josefská 1, Malá Strana ⏰ 6pm-3am Ⓜ Malostranská

Bombay Cocktail Bar (4, E2)
Upstairs from Rasoi (p77), this is an elegant, laid-back place to sip a sidecar or a Tom Collins or two. The cocktail list goes on and on, and the nightly DJ is more than happy to take requests.
☎ 222 324 040 ✉ Dlouhá 13, Staré Město ⏰ 4pm-4am Ⓜ Náměstí Republiky

Boulder Bar (4, E6)
Sporty-looking pub with an unusual take on interior decor, with oars and kayaks dangling from the ceiling. If it all makes you feel like climbing the walls, you can – there's an artificial climbing wall at the back for you to work up a thirst (70Kč per two hours, shoe rental 20Kč).
☎ 222 231 244 🖳 www .boulder.cz ✉ V jámě 6, Nové Město ⏰ bar 10am-midnight Mon-Fri, noon-midnight Sat & Sun; climbing wall 3-10pm Ⓜ Muzeum

Jo's Bar (5, C3)
Longstanding backpacker haunt, upstairs from the Garáž club (p86), with an ever-crowded little bar-restaurant and satellite TV. Nachos, burritos and pasta dishes are served to accompany the beer.
☎ 257 451 271 ✉ Malostranské náměstí 7, Malá Strana ⏰ 11am-late Ⓜ Malostranská

Legends Sports Bar (7, D2)
With 16 TV screens showing everything from British football to boxing, this place can easily claim to be Prague's biggest and most popular sports bar. It isn't that big, however, and gets very crowded very quickly. Huge drinks list, lots of burgers, and all-day breakfasts.
☎ 224 895 404 ✉ www .legends.cz ✉ Týnský dvůr 1, Staré Město ⏰ 11am-1am Sun-Wed, 11am-3am Thu-Sat Ⓜ Náměstí Republiky

Monarch Vinný Sklep (4, D5)
Kick back and relax with a few glasses of quality vino at this upmarket wine bar. The list is enormous, with producers from Luxembourg to New Zealand represented. There's also a big menu of French cheeses to nibble while you imbibe.
☎ 224 239 602 ✉ www .monarch.cz ✉ Na Perštýně 15, Staré Město ⏰ 3pm-late Mon-Sat Ⓜ Národní Třída

Na Schůdkách (4, G2)
This quiet bar and restaurant serves some less common beers, such as Starobrno (19Kč per 500mL), and cheap food including goulash and steaks, though the menu is only in Czech. It has Internet access too (1Kč per minute).
☎ 222 310 184 ✉ Zlatnická 11, Nové Město ⏰ 11am-midnight Ⓜ Náměstí Republiky

Ocean Drive (4, E2)
There's a touch of American West Coast chic about this slightly precious cocktail bar for local fashionistas and friends. It's a wonderfully stylish place, though, and a pleasant place to while away the evening over a gimlet. There's a predictably huge range of excellent cocktails.
☎ 224 819 089 ✉ V kolkovně 7, Staré Město ⏰ 4pm-2am Ⓜ Staroměstská

O'Che's (7, A3)
The only revolutionary spirits you'll find in this 'Cuban-Irish' pub are on the shelves behind the paraphernalia-riddled bar. Caters to sports-starved drinkers, who need a dose of football or rugby with their Guinness. Hearty English breakfasts, omelettes and steaks are also served.

PIVO & VINO

Czech beer *(pivo)* is famous worldwide, and rightly so – it's among the very best you'll find anywhere. Czechs are the biggest beer-drinkers on the planet, downing on average 160L per person each year. The most popular local brews are Pilsener Urquell, Staropramen, Krušovice, Gambrinus and Budvar. There are also many excellent microbreweries producing high-quality beers.

The 10, 12 or other numeral designated to beers along with a degree symbol thankfully doesn't represent alcohol content. It's a measurement of the density of the prefermentation beer mixture – 10° beers are dark beers, while 12° are generally lighter.

Czech wine *(vino)*, meanwhile, is barely heard of outside the country, since nearly all of it is consumed at home. Most of the Czech Republic's wine comes from Moravia, although Bohemia also produces modest amounts. Frankovka and Svatovavřínecké are the leading red-grape varieties, while Müller Thurgau is the most popular white.

☎ 222 221 178 🖳 www
.oches.com ✉ Liliová 14,
Staré Město 🕙 10am-1am
Ⓜ Staroměstská

Papas Bar (4, D4)

Sip cocktails with all the
beautiful people in this upmarket lounge bar. There's
a big wine list to choose
from, and you can also
munch your way through
light meals such as salads
and risottos.
☎ 222 222 229 🖳 www
.papasbar.cz ✉ Betlémské
náměstí 8, Staré Město
🕙 noon-2am Mon-Sat,
noon-1am Sun Ⓜ Národní
Třída

Pivnice Na Ovocném trhu (7, E2)

If the tiny, gloomy interior
of this old-fashioned pub is
not to your liking, there are
plenty of seats out on the
cobblestones, complete with
festive parasols. It's a rather
relaxing spot, watched over
by the Estates Theatre (see
p31 and p92 for details),
and there's a menu of the
usual Czech dishes.
☎ 224 211 955
✉ Ovocný trh 17, Staré
Město 🕙 11am-10pm
Ⓜ Náměstí Republiky

Pivnice U Sveti Tomáše (4, A3)

Descend into the depths
of this medieval vaulted
cellar for an atmospheric
beer-glugging session
seated at long wooden
tables. The nightly brass
bands give the place a more
touristy turn. Meals, of the
pork knuckle and goulash
persuasion, are available.
☎ 257 531 835
✉ Letenská 12, Malá Strana

Gleaming copper beer vats at Pivovarský Dům

🕙 11.30am-midnight
Ⓜ Malostranská

Pivovarský Dům (6, C5)

Adorned with vintage
brewery artefacts and a
pair of gleaming copper
vats, this friendly microbrewery and restaurant offers a
big menu of Czech favourites
such as venison, trout
and duck. It's the unusual
house beers, including
coffee, banana and nettle
varieties, that are the real
attraction though. Its
champagne beer is
particularly good.
☎ 296 216 666 🖳 www
.gastroinfo.cz/pivodum
✉ Lípová 15 (entry on
Ječná), Nové Město 🕙 11am-
11.30pm Ⓜ IP Pavlova

Propaganda (4, C6)

This small, busy neigh-
bourhood pub, strewn
with abstract sculptures,
attracts a youngish crowd,
half of whom seem to
gather permanently around
the table-football in the
back room.
☎ 224 932 285
✉ Pštrossova 29, Nové

Město 🕙 3pm-2am Mon-
Fri, 5pm-2am Sat & Sun
Ⓜ Národní Třída

Rocky O'Reilly's (4, F6)

No prizes for guessing, yes
this is an 'Irish' pub (they
serve Guinness and have
photos of James Joyce and
George Bernard Shaw on the
wall), and it's a big hit with
boisterous British and Irish
visitors. There's a separate
restaurant serving hearty but
slightly overpriced 'pub grub'.
🖳 www.rockyoreillys.cz
✉ Štěpánská 32, Nové
Město 🕙 10am-1am
Ⓜ Muzeum

Tlustá Koala (4, F3)

The 'Fat Koala' is a friendly,
British-style pub, complete
with dartboards, hunting
prints, and lots of polished
wood and brass, however
most of the clientele seems
to be local. The big res-
taurant in the back serves
traditional Czech food, and
you can eat in the bar too.
☎ 222 245 401
✉ Senovážná 8, Nové Město
🕙 noon-1am Ⓜ Náměstí
Republiky

Tlustá Myš (4, A5)
The subterranean 'Fat Mouse' pub is very much a local bar, with a couple of small rooms with long tables for those sociable evening drinks. The extensive list of inventive cocktails may keep you longer than you anticipated, and there are also small exhibitions of local art.
☎ 605 282 506
✉ Všehrdova 19, Malá Strana ⏰ 11am-midnight Mon-Thu, 2pm-1am Fri & Sat, 3-11pm Sun Ⓜ Národní Třída, then tram 6, 9, 22, 23, 57 or 58

U Pinkasů (4, E5)
Opened in 1843, this seemingly forever-full old pub was the first to serve Pilsner Urquell, and is something of a local institution. Waiters will plonk a beer in front of you whether you ask for it or not, and traditional Czech food is also served. Grab a seat on the rear patio.
☎ 221 111 150 ✉ Jungmannovo náměstí 16, Nové Město ⏰ 9am-4am Ⓜ Můstek

Víno Blatel (4, D4)
This friendly little wine bar is patronised almost exclusively by locals, and has a refreshingly down-to-earth atmosphere, as well as down-to-earth prices. Sit at one of the three tables with a glass of chilled Müller Thurgau and relax.
☎ 224 225 860 ✉ Michalská 51, Staré Město ⏰ 10am-7pm Mon-Fri Ⓜ Můstek

CLUBS

Duplex (4, F5)
Duplex is one of Prague's bigger and flashier discos, with huge sweaty dance halls filled with local teenagers and stag-party stragglers. The 6th-floor terrace restaurant has great views.
☎ 224 232 319 🖥 www .duplexduplex.cz ✉ Václavské náměstí 21, Nové Město ⓔ vary ⏰ 9pm-6am Thu-Sat Ⓜ Můstek

Futurum (6, B5)
Techno and garage music dominates at Futurum, along with more mainstream 1980s and '90s hits. It also has record launches, alternative bands and various DJs in attendance, and features lots of metal and exposed brick walls.
☎ 257 328 571 🖥 www .musicbar.cz ✉ Zborovská 7, Smíchov ⓔ 80-130Kč ⏰ 9pm-3am Ⓜ Anděl

Garáž (5, C3)
Dark two-level bar-club downstairs at Jo's Bar (p84), usually well patronised by backpackers until the wee hours, with an attendance peak during happy hour (6pm to 10pm).
☎ 257 533 342 ✉ Malostranské náměstí 7, Malá Strana ⓔ free ⏰ 6pm-5am Ⓜ Malostranská

Karlovy Lázně (4, C4)
Four-level 'superclub' where you can watch live bands at ground level (MCM Café), dance to classic disco on one (Discothéque), rock to 1960s and '70s music on two (Kaleidoskop), or bypass them all and head for the house and techno on three (Paradogs).
☎ 222 220 502 🖥 www .karlovylazne.cz ✉ Novotného lávka, Staré Město ⓔ 50-120Kč ⏰ 9pm-5am Ⓜ Staroměstská

Klub 007 (6, B4)
Hardly the kind of place Bond, James Bond, might frequent. This grungy student hang-out, in an inconspicuous location under the stairs on the eastern side of dorm block 7, plays very, very loud punk, death metal, ska and hip-hop.
☎ 257 211 439 🖥 www .klub007strahov.cz ✉ block 7,

Strahov dormitory complex, Chaloupekého 7, Strahov ⓔ 50-200Kč ⏱ 7.30pm-1am Tue-Sat Ⓜ Dejvická, then bus 143, 149 or 217 to Chaloupekého

Mecca (6, E2)
This ultrafashionable hang-out is done out with stark colours, space-age vinyl couches, and other such fashion statements. Many of the beautiful people, models and aspiring wannabees flock to Mecca's industrial-chic club to dance to house, drum 'n' bass and techno.
☎ 283 870 522 💻 www .mecca.cz ✉ U Průhonu 3, Holešovice ⓔ 150-250Kč ⏱ 11am-10pm Mon-Thu, 11-6am Fri, noon-6am Sat; club from 10pm Ⓜ Nádraží Holešovice

Meloun (7, C4)
This dark cellar bar and club attracts a largely local, youthful crowd, especially for the weekend Czech pop discos, when you'll be lucky to squeeze through the

door. Western pop plays on Monday, while Tuesday is karaoke night.
☎ 224 230 126 💻 www .meloun.cz ✉ Michalská 12, Staré Město ⓔ Mon, Wed & Thu free, Tue, Fri & Sat 60-100Kč ⏱ 7pm-3am Mon-Sat Ⓜ Můstek

Radost FX (3, A2)
Prague's slickest and shiniest club is the place to mingle with the city's beautiful people. Its bohemian lounge is appealingly decked out in mosaic-topped tables and sumptuous sofas, while the downstairs club features top local DJs. Every third Saturday is gay night.
☎ 603 181 500 💻 www .radostfx.cz ✉ Bělehradská 120, Vinohrady ⓔ 100-250Kč ⏱ 10pm-5am Ⓜ IP Pavlova

Roxy (4, F2)
The expansive floor of this ramshackle old theatre has seen many a hard-edged DJ and band over the years,

plus plenty of experimental fare in the form of drama, dance and short films. All shadowy nooks and crannies usually fill up quickly once the doors open.
☎ 224 826 296 💻 www .roxy.cz ✉ Dlouhá 33, Josefov ⓔ 80-250Kč, Mon free ⏱ 1pm-late Ⓜ Náměstí Republiky

JAZZ

AghaRTA Jazz Centrum (7, D3)
Prague's leading jazz club relocated to this smoky subterranean venue in 2004. It has an innovative programme of jazz, swing and blues, and a mixed crowd of locals and visitors regularly pack it to its stone vaulted ceiling. There's also a shop selling new and secondhand CDs (p60).
☎ 222 211 275 💻 www .agharta.cz ✉ Železná 16, Staré Město ⓔ 100Kč ⏱ 7pm-1am, shows 9pm-midnight Ⓜ Můstek

FOLLOW THE GREEN FAIRY
With its *belle époque*, demimonde associations, absinthe has made a comeback in Prague as the spirit of choice of alternative trendsetters. Popularly known as the 'green fairy', absinthe is a powerful concoction (70% alcohol content) flavoured with wormwood, and it was consumed in huge quantities across Europe (especially in France) in the late 19th and early 20th centuries. Leading artists, writers and other louche libertines of the period were attracted by its potency, vibrant green hue and ritual preparation, but it had bothersome side-effects, such as blindness and death, which eventually led to it being banned.

Absinthe was legalised again in the Czech Republic in the 1990s and has become something of a cultural icon, with several brands available.

PLAYING SOLO

Entertaining your sole self in Prague is easy and uncomplicated. Cafés and bars are invariably dotted with unaccompanied Czechs and foreigners enjoying their own company or the qualities of a good book, newspaper or menu, while live music venues also have their share of self-possessed attendees.

Though wandering into a crowded beer hall on your own may at first appear an intimidating exercise, just head for a space at a less-populated bench and inquire *'Je tu volno'* ('Is it free?') before sitting down. You may even find yourself waved over to a spare spot with companionable, refreshment-flowing consequences.

Jazz Boat (4, D1)
This vessel's 2½-hour Vltava-cruising concerts featuring blues, swing and Czech jazz are pitched forcefully at tourists, but a varied selection of local outfits also perform here. Simple food and drinks can be had at the onboard restaurant at extra cost.
☎ 731 183 180 🖳 www
.jazzboat.cz ✉ Pier No 5, under Čechův most, Josefov
€ 590Kč 🕑 8.30-11pm
Tue-Sun Ⓜ Staroměstská

Metropolitan Jazz Club (4, E6)
Basement jazz 'n' blues haunt, with easily digestible

ragtime and swing compositions. There's a preference for substance over style, hence the plain-tiled floor and lack of adornment.
☎ 224 947 777 ✉ Jungmannova 14, Nové Město
€ 100Kč 🕑 6pm-1am Mon-Fri, 7pm-1am Sat & Sun; shows 9pm-12.30am
Ⓜ Národní Třída

Reduta (4, D5)
Prague's oldest jazz club has an intimate setting, with well-attired patrons squeezing into tiered seats and lounges to soak up the big-band, swing and Dixieland atmosphere. Can oversell tickets, causing a last-minute scramble for seating.
☎ 224 912 246 🖳 www
.redutajazzclub.cz
✉ Národní třída 20, Nové Město € 280-300Kč
🕑 box office from 3pm Mon-Fri, from 7pm Sat & Sun; shows 9pm-3am
Ⓜ Národní Třída

U Malého Glena (5, C4)
Melange of jazz styles (and blues) served up nightly at this informal venue, including modern, Latin and vocal. Jam sessions are held regularly here, and amateurs are welcome. If you'd like to stay after hours, the club

has a few simple hotel rooms upstairs (1950Kč).
☎ 290 003 967 🖳 www
.malyglen.cz ✉ Karmelitská 23, Malá Strana € 100-150Kč 🕑 10am-2am; shows 9pm-12.30am Sun-Thu, 10pm-1.30am Sat & Sun
Ⓜ Malostranská

Ungelt Jazz & Blues Club (7, D2)
This popular, if poky, 15th-century vault venue can be crammed with people attracted by 'Free Jazz' signage around the Old Town Square, but it appears an admission price is usually charged. Jazz fusion and blues dominate the nightly programme.
☎ 224 895 748 🖳 www
.jazzblues.cz ✉ Týnská ulička 2, Staré Město
€ 120Kč 🕑 pub noon-midnight, jazz club 8pm-late, shows 9pm-midnight
Ⓜ Náměstí Republiky

U Staré Paní (7, C4)
Located in the bowels of the hotel of the same name, this well-established jazz club caters to all levels of musical appreciation. There's a varied programme of modern jazz, soul, blues and Latin rhythms, and a nightly DJ spot from midnight on.
☎ 603 551 680 🖳 www
.jazzlounge.cz ✉ Michalská 9,

Staré Město € 150–200Kč
🕐 7pm–2am, shows 9pm–
midnight, World Music Party
from midnight Ⓜ Můstek

ROCK, BLUES & FOLK

Dlabačov Hall (6, A4)
The Czech Song and
Dance Ensemble, formed
in 1947, is the republic's
sole professional folk
performance troupe, though
other 'folklore' events are
irregularly and mostly
less impressively staged
elsewhere.
☎ 233 373 475 ✉ Hotel
Pyramida, Bělohorská 24,
Střešovice € 450Kč
🕐 shows at 8.30pm Mon–
Sat Apr–Nov Ⓜ Hradčanská,
then tram 8 to Malovanka

Lucerna Music Bar (4, F5)
Nostalgia rules at this atmospheric old theatre, with
anything from Beatles and

Red Hot Chilli Peppers tribute
bands to Czech blues, rock or
folk acts on stage. The 1980s
and '90s 'video parties' are
particularly popular, while
other offerings include R & B
on Thursday.
☎ 224 215 957 🖳 www
.musicbar.cz ✉ Lucerna
Passage, Vodičkova 36,
Nové Město € 80–165Kč
🕐 8pm–3am, shows from
9pm Ⓜ Můstek

Palác Akropolis (6, E4)
Labyrinthine entertainment
palace with a wealth of
alternative talent (local and
international) on show in
its various performance
spaces, from Macedonian
gypsy bands to string quartets and hip-hop. Has a good
café and restaurant too.
☎ 296 330 911 🖳 www
.palacakropolis.cz
✉ Kubelíkova 27, Žižkov
€ 150–300Kč 🕐 café
10am–midnight Mon–Fri,

4pm–midnight Sat & Sun;
club 4pm–4am Ⓜ Jiřího z
Poděbrad

Red Hot & Blues (7, F1)
This place is more of a
Tex-Mex dinner show than
a blues or jazz club, but still
pleases tourists with its
mixture of live music and
platefuls of Creole and Cajun
cooking. There's live music
most nights.
☎ 222 323 364
✉ Jakubská 12, Staré Město
€ free 🕐 9am–11pm,
shows 7–10pm Ⓜ Náměstí
Republiky

Rock Café (4, D5)
Over-commercialised to
the hilt and loving it, this
place has a cinema, an art
gallery and an auditorium.
Check out 'Free Puerto' night
(Tuesday in summer), a
blend of bhangra, flamenco,
reggae and 'songs of Mongo-
lian herdsmen'.
☎ 224 914 416 🖳 www
.rockcafe.cz ✉ Národní třída
20, Nové Město € 50–100Kč
🕐 10am–3am Mon–Fri,
5pm–3am Sat, 5pm–1am
Sun; shows at 8.30pm
Ⓜ Národní Třída

THEATRE

All Colours Theatre (7, D3)
One of the top black-light
theatre exponents, putting
on bizarre and colourful
shows with outstanding
special effects accompanying
the music and dancing. You
also get a tour of the gallery.
☎ 221 610 173
🖳 www.blacktheatre.cz
✉ Rytířská 31, Nové Město
€ 590/450Kč 🕐 box office
10am–9pm; shows at 8.30pm
Ⓜ Můstek ♿

Let the magic begin

Black Light Theatre of Jiří Srnec (4, D5)
Based in the Reduta theatre (p88), this was the original black-light outfit, formed in 1961. Its programme is full of surreal and fantastical tableaux, plus adaptations of classic tales such as *Peter Pan*. Performances also take place at the City Library (7, B2; Marianské náměstí).
☎ 602 291 572 🖳 www .blacktheatresrnec.cz ✉ Národní Třída 20, Nové Město € 490Kč 🕐 box office from 3pm Mon-Fri, from 7pm Sat & Sun; performances at 7.30pm Ⓜ Národní Třída ♿

Celetná Theatre (7, E2)
In an arcade running between Celetná and Štupartská, the Celetná stages mainly Czech drama, as well as foreign works, such as those by Shakespeare, which have been translated into Czech.
☎ 222 326 843 ✉ Celetná 17, Staré Město € up to 250Kč 🕐 box office 1-7.30pm; usually at least 1 show daily at 7.30pm Ⓜ Náměstí Republiky

Goja Music Hall (6, D2)
Striking glass pyramid-shaped theatre in the Fairgrounds hosting the usual big international shows and hit musicals such as *Les Misérables* and *Miss Saigon* (in Czech).
☎ 220 103 621 🖳 www .goja.cz ✉ Fairgrounds (Výstaviště), Holešovice € 650Kč Ⓜ Nádraží Holešovice, then tram 5, 12, 17, 53 or 54 to Výstaviště ♿

Image Theatre (7, C2)
Creative black-light theatre, with pantomime, contem-porary dance and video – not to mention liberal doses of slapstick – to tell their stories. The staging can be very effective, but the atmosphere is often dictated by audience reaction.
☎ 222 329 191 🖳 www .imagetheatre.cz ✉ Pařížská třída 4, Staré Město € 400Kč 🕐 box office 9am-8pm; performances at 8pm Ⓜ Staroměstská

Laterna Magika (4, C5)
Since its first cutting-edge performance of music, dance and film at the 1958 Brussels World Fair, Laterna Magika has been highly successful both at home and abroad. Shows, such as 'The Legend of the Argonauts' and 'The Wonderful Circus' employ an

---

GLOWING ACTS
'Black-light theatre' is one of those typically surreal, off-the-wall experiences that Praguers seem to delight in. Developed in the city more than four decades ago, it's an innovative mixture of pantomime, dance, drama, film projections and puppetry performed in front of a black backdrop by ultraviolet-illuminated actors and objects all dressed in phosphorescent garb. Classic children's stories, and myths and legends are favoured topics, while more contemporary, avant-garde subject matter is becoming popular too.

A growing number of places are presenting this theatrical genre in Prague. The more interesting and entertaining companies include the Black Light Theatre of Jiří Srnec (above), Image Theatre (above) and All Colours Theatre (p89).

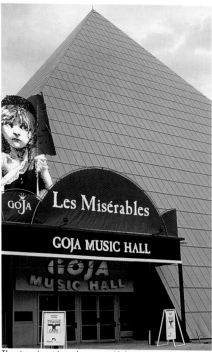

The stage is set in a glass pyramid theatre

innovative mixture of live acting and projected images that continues to draw the crowds.
☎ 224 931 482 🖥 www .laterna.cz ✉ Národní třída 4, Nové Město €️ 680Kč ⏰ box office 10am-8pm Mon-Sat; performances at 8pm Mon-Sat Ⓜ Národní Třída

National Marionette Theatre (7, B2)
Loudly touted as the longest-running classical marionette show in Prague, *Don Giovanni* is an operatic, life-sized marionette extravaganza that has spawned several imitators around town. But be warned, younger kids'

interests may begin to wane quite early during this two-hour show.
☎ 224 819 323 🖥 www .mozart.cz ✉ Žatecká 1, Staré Město €️ 490/390Kč ⏰ box office 10am-8pm; performances at 8pm Ⓜ Staroměstská ♿

Spiral Theatre (6, D2)
In the sprawling Fairgrounds in Holešovice, this tall black industrial rotunda of a building hosts various shows, including productions of Shakespeare and local and international music acts.
☎ 220 103 624 ✉ Fairgrounds (Výstaviště), Holešovice €250-500Kč ⏰ box office 3-7pm Tue-

Sun Ⓜ Nádraží Holešovice, then tram 5, 12, 17, 53 or 54 to Výstaviště

Ta Fantastika (7, A3)
Established in New York in 1981 by expat Czech Petr Kratochvil. Shows are based on classic children's literature such as *The Little Prince* and *Aspects of Alice*. Has won international acclaim.
☎ 222 221 366 🖥 www .tafantastika.cz ✉ Karlova 8, Staré Město €️ 650Kč ⏰ box office 11am-9.30pm; performances at 7pm Jul-Aug, & 9.30pm, Ⓜ Staroměstská ♿

Theatre on the Balustrade (7, A4)
Immerse yourself in Czech-language drama at the theatre where Václav Havel honed his skills as a playwright four decades ago. This 'off-Národní' theatre (Divadlo Na zábradlí) dabbled in absurdism early in its existence and now plays host to a variety of slightly more contemporary material.
☎ 222 222 026 🖥 www .nazabradli.cz ✉ Anenské náměstí 5, Staré Město €️ 90-250Kč ⏰ box office 2-7pm Ⓜ Staroměstská ♿

CLASSICAL MUSIC, OPERA & BALLET

Bertramka (6, B5)
Mozart stayed in this villa during his visits to Prague. Now it has been restored and it is used as a museum and charming venue for classical concerts, held in the salon and gardens.

JUST THE TICKET

Even up to 30 minutes before a performance starts, you can often still get a ticket at the box office. When booking ahead is advised or you have your rear end primed for a particular seat, the following computerised ticket agencies can help you out – note that you're probably looking at a 10% to 15% mark-up and some agencies don't take credit cards.

Bohemia Ticket (7, C3; ☎ 224 227 832; www.bohemiaticket.cz; Malé náměstí 13, Staré Město)

Bohemia Ticket (7, F3; ☎ 224 215 031; Na Příkopě 16, Staré Město)

FOK (7, F2; ☎ 222 002 336; www.fok.cz; U Obecního domu 2, Nové Město) Mainly Prague Symphony Orchestra tickets.

Ticketpro (7, C1; ☎ 224 816 020; www.ticketpro.cz; Salvátorská 10, Josefov; ☟ closed Sat & Sun)

Ticketpro (7, D4; ☎ 221 610 162; Řytířská 12, Staré Město)

String quartets, wind trios and so on provide the notes. ☎ 257 318 461 🖳 www .bertramka.cz 🖳 Mozartova 169 € Smíchov concerts 370-450Kč, museum 110/50Kč ☟ concerts at 5pm & 7pm Apr-Oct; museum 9.30am-6pm Apr-Oct, 9.30am-5pm Nov-Mar Ⓜ Anděl, then tram 10 to Kartouzská

Estates Theatre (7, D3)
This Stavovské Divadlo is the oldest theatre in Prague, and famed as the place where Mozart conducted the premiere of *Don Giovanni*, a touristy version of which is staged by the Opera Mozart company each summer. The rest of the year sees operatic and ballet productions. ☎ 224 901 638 ✉ Ovocný trh 1, Staré Město € 190-1990Kč ☟ box office at Kolowrat Palace (7, D3; Ovocný trh 6) 10am-6pm Mon-Fri, 10am-12.30pm Sat & Sun; theatre box office opens 30min before performances Ⓜ Můstek ♿ good, plus facilities for the hearing-impaired

Municipal House (7, F2)
Smetana Hall, centrepiece of the stunning Obecní Dům, is the city's biggest concert hall (with a seating capacity for 1500), and main venue for the Prague Symphony Orchestra. Other halls in Prague host regular one-hour concerts, ranging from Vivaldi's *Four Seasons* to the *Best of Gershwin*. ☎ 222 002 101 🖳 www .fok.cz ✉ náměstí Republiky 5, Staré Město € 50-1200Kč ☟ box office 10am-6pm &

also opens 1hr before concerts Mon-Fri Ⓜ Náměstí Republiky

National Theatre (4, C5)
The glorious, golden-roofed centrepiece of Czech performing arts institutions, Národní Divadlo is credited with providing a forum for the emancipation of Czech culture. Traditional opera, drama and ballet performances share the stage with more avant-garde works by contemporary composers and dramatists.

The queue stops here

Memories are made of this — a ferry ride at dusk on the Vltava River

☎ 114 901 448 💻 www
.narodni-divadlo.cz
✉ Národní třída 2, Nové
Město € 200-900Kč
⏰ box office behind
theatre 10am-6pm, evening
theatre box office opens
45min before performances,
closed end Jun–mid-Aug
Ⓜ Národní Třída

Prague State Opera
(4, G6)
The impressive neo-rococo
home of the Prague State
Opera (Státní Opera Praha) is
a glorious setting for operatic
standards and ballet. The
annual Verdi Festival takes
place in late August/Sep-
tember, while more unusual
productions have included
Scott Joplin's *Treemonisha*
and Leoncavallo's rarely
staged version of *La Bohème*.
☎ 224 227 266 💻 www
.opera.cz ✉ Wilsonova 4,
Nové Město € opera 400-
1200Kč, ballet 200-550Kč
⏰ box office 10am-5.30pm
Mon-Fri, 10am-noon &

1-5.30pm Sat & Sun,
closed end Jun–mid-Aug
Ⓜ Muzeum

Rudolfinum (4, C2)
Within the imposing
neo-Renaissance Rudolfinum
you'll find the colonnade-
lined Dvořák Hall. This
magnificent concert hall is
the performance base for
the world-renowned Czech
Philharmonic Orchestra,
and hosts various concert
programmes and festivals
year-round, including the
Prague Proms.
☎ 227 059 352 💻 www
.rudolfinum.cz ✉ náměstí
Jana Palacha 1, Josefov
€ 150-900Kč ⏰ box office
10am-12.30pm & 1.30-6pm
Mon-Fri Ⓜ Staroměstská

Vinohrady Theatre (3, B2)
This grand building (Divadlo
Na Vinohradech) dates from
1909, and is a popular venue
for ballet and classical music.
During the summer months,
it stages opera performances,

while the main Prague
State Opera is closed.
☎ 224 257 601 ✉ náměstí
Míru 7, Vinohrady €500-
1200Kč ⏰ box office 11am-
7pm Mon-Fri, 1-7pm Sat
Sep-Jun, 3-8pm Jul-Aug
Ⓜ Náměstí Míru

CINEMAS

Cinema City (6, E4)
Modern multiplex on the top
floor of the Palác Flóra shopping mall (p54), showing recent Hollywood releases with
Czech subtitles. Also here is
the Oskar IMAX screen, which
shows a limited selection of
3-D features.
☎ 255 742 021 💻 www
.cinemacity.cz ✉ Palác
Flóra, Vinohradská 149, Vinohrady € 159/100, IMAX
159-179Kč ⏰ box office
from 11.30am Ⓜ Flora ♿

Kino Světozor (4, E5)
The emphasis here is on
Czech and European art-
house films, mostly with

MOVING PICTURES

Czech film-making blossomed from 1963 to 1968, when graduates of a communist-run film academy side-stepped censorship. Among them was Miloš Forman, who produced 1963's *Černý Petr* (Black Peter), and Jiří Menzel, whose *Ostre sledované vlaky* (Closely Observed Trains; 1966) won an Oscar. Jan Svěrák directed two pivotal films: *Kolja* (1996) and *Tmavomodrý svět* (The Dark-Blue World; 2001), about Czech pilots in WWII. David Ondříček released the acclaimed *Samotáři* in 2000, a year that also saw Jan Hrebejk's Academy Award–nominated *Musíme si pomáhat* (Divided We Fall).

International movies that have been substantially shot in the Czech capital include Forman's *Amadeus*, Barbara Streisand's *Yentl*, Brian de Palma's *Mission Impossible* and Stephen Norrington's *The League of Extraordinary Gentlemen*.

English subtitles, though not always. Classic English-language films and occasional mainstream movies are also shown, with documentaries on Mondays.
☎ 224 946 824 🖳 www .kinosvetozor.cz ✉ Vodičkova 41, Nové Město € 100Kč ☽ box office from 10.30am Ⓜ Můstek

Kino Perštýn (4, D5)
Downstairs cinema that forgoes those boring old rows of seats for a sociable scattering of tables and chairs. You can smoke in the next-door bar, but only drinks (and not fumes) can accompany you into the cinema. English- and foreign-language films with Czech subtitles.
☎ 221 668 432 ✉ Na Perštýně 6, Staré Město € 80-130Kč ☽ box office from 4pm Ⓜ Národní Třída

Lucerna (4, F5)
A miscellany of new and old Czech-, European- and English-language films are screened at this atmospheric one-theatre venue, so it's a matter of luck as to what's on when you're in town. You'll find it under the upside-down horse.

☎ 224 216 972 ✉ Lucerna Passage, Vodičkova 36, Nové Město € 99Kč ☽ box office 10am-noon, 1-7.30pm & 8-9.15pm Ⓜ Můstek

MAT Studio (6, C4)
Former TV studio and private-screening venue turned cool cinema, where film types sip espressos and wine in the celluloid-decorated downstairs bar-club or the arty upstairs bistro. Czech films with English subtitles and vice versa.
☎ 224 915 765 🖳 www .mat.cz ✉ Charles Square 19, Nové Město €95Kč ☽ 11am-midnight Mon-Fri,

2pm-midnight Sat & Sun Ⓜ Karlovo Náměstí ♿

Palace Cinema (7, F3)
Ten screens of the latest Hollywood offerings, normally in English with Czech subtitles, plus the odd European or Czech film, in one brightly lit complex. There's another branch inside the Nový Smíchov shopping centre (p54).
☎ 257 181 212 🖳 www .palacecinemas.cz ✉ Na příkopě 22, Nové Město € 159/119Kč ☽ box office 11.30am-9pm Mon-Fri, 11.30am-10.30pm Sat & Sun Ⓜ Náměstí Republiky ♿

Summer Movie Theatre
(4, B5)

Alfresco summer-only film screenings under the trees on Střelecký Ostrov. It's an informal setting, with recent and classic English-language movies on show at irregular intervals. Pick up a timetable at the Travellers' Hostel on the island (p102).

🖥 www.strelak.cz
✉ Střelecký Ostrov, Malá Strana 💶 80Kč ⏰ screenings at 9.30pm 🚊 6, 9, 22, 23, 57 or 58

GAY & LESBIAN PRAGUE

Club Stella (3, C3)

Popular small gay bar and café in Vinohrady. It's a friendly, laid-back place with a cosy cocktail lounge frequented mostly by locals. You'll need to ring the doorbell to get in.

☎ 224 257 869 ✉ Lužická 10, Vinohrady ⏰ 8pm-5am
Ⓜ Náměstí Míru

Friends (4, C5)

Recently relocated, Friends is probably Prague's most buzzing gay club, offering various theme nights Czech pop, '70s disco and DJ parties. It also hosts big events such as the 'Mr Czech' contest. Check the website for the latest programme.

☎ 224 236 772 🖥 www.friends-prague.cz
✉ Bartolomějská 11, Staré Město ⏰ 6pm-5am
Ⓜ Národní Třída

Gejzeer (3, B1)

Prague's biggest gay and lesbian club draws an equally big crowd to its two bars and disco. Besides the usual dance and video-related activities, Gejzeer seems keen to play matchmaker by offering 'meet a partner' nights and its equally euphemistic 'darkroom'.

☎ 222 516 036 🖥 www.gayzeer.cz ✉ Vinohradská 40, Vinohrady 💶 Thu free, Fri 100Kč, Sat 150Kč
⏰ 8pm-4am Thu, 9pm-6am Fri & Sat Ⓜ Náměstí Míru

Maler (3, B1)

This small café-club attracts a mixed crowd during the week. It hosts lesbian discos on Friday and Saturday nights, plus lesbian parties.

☎ 222 013 116 ✉ Blanická 28, Vinohrady 💶 Sun-Thu free, Fri & Sat 50Kč ⏰ 9am-11pm Mon-Thu, 9am-4am Fri & Sat, 1-10pm Sun
Ⓜ Náměstí Míru

Pivnice U Rudolfa (4, F6)

Intimate gay pub with cosy subterranean surrounds, just a brief stroll from the Muzeum metro. The Pivnice U Rudolfa is popular with older locals and gets considerably livelier late at night.

☎ 605 872 492 ✉ Mezibranská 3, Nové Město
💶 free ⏰ 4pm-2am
Ⓜ Muzeum

Termix (3, C1)

Industrial chic is the style choice at Termix, which features lots of steel, glass and a car sticking out of one wall. DJs play house and techno, and there's a convivial cocktail bar.

☎ 222 710 462
🖥 www.club-termix.cz
✉ Třebízského 4a, Vinohrady 💶 free ⏰ 8pm-5am
Wed-Sun Ⓜ Náměstí Míru

SPORT

Prague International Marathon

The annual 42km Prague International Marathon first hit the streets in 1989 and now attracts more foreigners than locals. The full run (from Old Town Square around Josefov, over Charles Bridge, south down Malá Strana and then back up to the square) is usually staged in the latter half of May, and a half-marathon is held mid-March.

Ice Hockey

Ice hockey (lední hokey) is the number-one national sport, and Czechs take it all very seriously. They've won numerous world titles, most recently the world championship in 2005. There are 14 teams in the national league, including the successful Sparta Praha and Slavia Praha. Catch the action at the T-Mobile Arena (6, D2) or the new Sazka Arena, built to host the 2004 world championship, which the Czechs lost.

Football

From August to December and February to June, AC Sparta Praha competes with itself to see how many points clear at the top of the ladder it will be by the domestic season's end. Although this team is occasionally pressed by rivals, including AC Slavia Praha, it usually makes a lot of vocal football (fotbal)

followers ecstatic by the competition's end. Catch a game at the AC Sparta Praha stadium.

Horse Racing

If racing (dostihy) is your scene, head to the horse-pounded turf at Chuchle závodiště. If you fancy a bet, races are generally run on Sundays from 2pm onwards between April and October. Tickets (70Kč) should be available at the racecourse (závodiště).

OFFICES & VENUES

AC Sparta Praha stadium (6, C3; ☎ 220 570 323; www.sparta.cz; Milady Horákové 98, Bubeneč; Ⓜ Hradčanská, tram 1, 8, 25, 26, 51 or 56)

Chuchle závodiště (☎ 257 941 431; Offices & Venues www.velka-chuchle.cz; Radotínská 69, Velká Chuchle; Ⓜ Smíchovské Nádraží, bus 129 or 172 to Chuchle závodiště)

HC Sparta Praha (6, D2; ☎ 266 727 443; www.hc sparta.cz; T-Mobile Arena, Za Elektrárnou 419, Bubeneč; Ⓜ Nádraží Holešovice, then tram 5, 12, 17, 53 or 54 to Výstaviště)

Sazka Arena (☎ 266 212 111; www.sazkaarena.cz; Ocerlařská 2, Vysočany; Ⓜ Českomoravská)

Prague International Marathon (☎ 224 919 209; www.pim.cz; 5th fl, Záhořanského 3, Nové Město; Ⓜ Karlovo Náměstí)

Fast, furious and freezing

Sleeping

Prague is one of Europe's most popular city-break destinations, and inundated with visitors year-round, but the busiest time is between April and October, and Easter, Christmas and New Year. Although the city already has hundreds of hotels, and new ones opening all the time, book as far ahead as possible during these times, and when your trip coincides with local and European public holidays.

Those hoping for dirt-cheap 'Eastern European' prices will be disappointed. These days, hotels in Prague charge the same kind of rates as big Western European cities, although bargains can still be found. The terms 'budget accommodation' and 'city centre' are almost mutually exclusive in Prague, but there are a number of decent modern hostels, catering mainly to backpackers scattered across the city, including some close to Old Town Square. The majority of budget places are outside Staré Město, mostly in southern Nové Město, east in Vinohrady, and north across the Vltava in Holešovice. *Penzións*, traditionally private boarding houses, can simply be very basic hotels; some of the genuine ones have homey surrounds, though these tend to be in outer areas.

ROOM RATES

The prices in this chapter indicate the cost per night of a standard double room in high season.

Deluxe	over 7500Kč
Top End	5500–7500Kč
Midrange	2500–5499Kč
Budget	under 2500Kč

Hotel Josef's (p98) understated elegance

Midrange options are often three-star hotels with their own restaurant, café and/or bar, and rooms equipped with bathroom, satellite TV, phone and minibar; some places are vastly overpriced for what's on offer. Meanwhile, there's no shortage of top-end choices stuffed full of classy eateries, grand fittings and business facilities.

Many city dwellers renovate and rent their apartments for short- or long-term stays. If you go for a flat in the more trampled bits of the Old Town, make sure your bedroom isn't facing the street – late-night revellers tend to treat the narrow streets as their own private karaoke studio. If you want to do your own home-hunting, head to your preferred area and look for *privát* or *Zimmer frei* (rooms for rent) signs.

Note that many hotels, especially top-end and deluxe ones, quote prices in euros, and even though the Czech Republic is not a member of the eurozone, you can still pay in the currency.

DELUXE

Andel's Hotel (6, B5)
The huge glassy edifice of Andel's offers four-star designer chic in the heart of up-and-coming Smíchov. There are 239 spacious rooms, with floor to ceiling windows and mod cons such as DVD and CD players, minibars and modems. Other facilities include a gym and hairdresser.
☎ 296 889 688 ☐ www .andelshotel.com ✉ Stroupežnického 21, Smíchov Ⓜ Anděl ✂

Bellagio Hotel (4, D2)
Bella Italia is the running theme at this modish hotel nestled in one of the quieter corners of Josefov, near the river. Rooms are suitably stylish, including four fitted for disabled guests, and there's a highly regarded restaurant in the cellar with a celebrity chef.
☎ 221 778 999 ☐ www .bellagiohotel.cz ✉ U milosrdných 2, Josefov Ⓜ Staroměstská, then tram 17 or 51 to Dvořakovo nábřeží ✂ Ristorante Isabella (p69)

Hotel Josef (4, F2)
With a stark white, minimalist vestibule more reminiscent of an exclusive Swiss clinic than a luxury hotel, this striking designer place has 110 soundproof rooms, including two for disabled guests. Also has a bar and business lounge, and the grooviest glass spiral staircase around.
☎ 221 700 111 ☐ www .hoteljosef.com ✉ Rybná 70, Staré Město Ⓜ Náměstí Republiky ✂

Hotel Paříž (7, F1-F2)
This Art Nouveau palace was built in 1904, and stands as a sumptuous memorial to the heady days of Alfons Mucha and Gustav Klimt, who each have plush suites named after them. Most rooms are furnished in bright, contemporary style, while the Royal Tower Suite has 360-degree views of Prague.
☎ 222 195 195 ☐ www .hotel-pariz.cz ✉ U Obec-ního domu 1, Staré Město Ⓜ Náměstí Republiky ✂ Sarah Bernhardt (p78)

Hotel Questenberk (2, B2)
Housed in a baroque 17th-century former monastic hospital, Questenberk is within easy strolling distance of the Castle and Strahov Monastery. The calm, church-like atmosphere has been retained, with added mod cons such as satellite TV and modems.
☎ 220 407 600 ☐ www .questenberk.cz ✉ Úvoz 15, Hradčany Ⓜ Malostran-ská, then tram 22 or 23 to Pohořelec ✂ Malý Buddha (p67) ♿

Hotel Residence Alchymist (5, B3)
This vivacious baroque palace offers large, sumptuously decorated rooms, though all the gilt stucco, swags and crystal chandeliers may be a touch overpowering for some. There's a welcoming spa, an atmospheric pool in the cellar and an art gallery.
☎ 257 286 011 ☐ www .alchymistresidence.com ✉ Tržiště 19, Malá Strana Ⓜ Malostranská ✂

Eye-catching Art Nouveau Hotel Paříž

Residence Nosticova
(5, C5)
Under the same management as Hotel Residence Alchymist, Nosticova is less gaudy with 10 individually decorated apartments with kitchenette. Original artworks grace the walls, while one suite has a grand piano.
☎ 257 312 513 ▯ www .nosticova.com ✉ Nosticova 1, Malá Strana Ⓜ Malostranská, then tram 12, 22, 23 or 57 to Hellichova ✕ Restaurant Alchymist (p70)

Residence Řetězová
(7, B3)
This lovely historic mansion has nine differently sized, and priced, apartments, some with fireplaces, kitchens and original painted beams. The largest are spread over two floors, and have great views.
☎ 222 221 800 ▯ www .residenceretezova.com ✉ Řetězová 9, Staré Město Ⓜ Staroměstská ✕ Ebel Coffee House (p75)

TOP END

Ametyst (3, B3)
This grand white edifice looks slightly out of scale on a very quiet Vinohrady backstreet

but it's a friendly, if somewhat somnolent, place, with bright, squeaky-clean and attractively furnished rooms. There's a sauna, a solarium and massage available for the travel-weary, and a couple of limousines to whisk you to and from the airport.
☎ 222 921 921 ▯ www .hotelametyst.cz ✉ Jana Masaryka 11, Vinohrady Ⓜ Náměstí Míru ✕ La Galleria; Vienna ⚱

Blue Key (4, A3)
Dating back to the 14th century, U Modrého Klíče currently wears a baroque makeover and offers quiet, restful rooms, some with original painted ceilings. The name comes from an old legend concerning a secret room opened with a special blue key, where, during a full moon, all dreams would come true. No promises these days though.
☎ 257 534 361 ▯ www .bluekey.cz ✉ Letenská 14, Malá Strana Ⓜ Malostranská, then tram 22 or 23

Carlo IV (4, H4)
Liveried doormen, a palmfilled atrium, sumptuous furnishings and impeccable

Hotel Questenberk

service are the hallmarks of luxury at this showy Italian chain hotel. There's a spa, pool, restaurant and cigar bar, and it's handy for the main train station.
☎ 224 593 111 ▯ www .boscolohotels.com ✉ Senovážné náměstí 13, Nové Město Ⓜ Hlavní Nádraží ✕ Box Block (p72)

Domus Henrici (2, C2)
Outside, you'd barely know this discrete little hotel was here. You'll have to ring the bell to gain admittance.

ACCOMMODATION AGENCIES
The following are some reputable accommodation agencies, covering everything from hostels to luxury hotels and private accommodation. Some agencies prefer you to pay first and then see a place, whereas you'll probably want it the other way around – if in doubt, be persistent.
AVE (4, H5; ☎ 251 091 111; www.avetravel.cz; ⊗ 'last minute' office at main train station 6am-11pm)
Estec (☎ 257 210 410; estec@jrc.cz)
Happy House Rentals (4, E5; ☎ 222 312 488; www.happyhouserentals.com; 1st fl Palác Langhans, Vodičkova 37, Nové Město)
Rentego (☎ 224 323 734; www.rentego.com)

Inside there are eight peaceful rooms with wonderful views, and facilities aimed at business travellers including fax machines, modems, 'business desks' and mini hi-fis.

☎ 220 511 369 🖳 www .hidden-places.com ✉ Loretánská 11, Hradčany 🅼 Malostranská, then tram 22 or 23 to Pohořec 🍽 U Labutí (p67) ♿

Hotel Ungelt (7, F2)

Unique and stylish, all-suite boutique hotel, right in the heart of the Old Town. Part of the hotel dates back to the 12th century, and it's an interesting mix of Gothic and Renaissance décor, with plenty of chandeliers and swept-back drapery. All suites have kitchens, although if you fancy a lie in, breakfast will be served to your room.

☎ 224 828 686 🖳 www .ungelt.cz ✉ Štupartská 1, Staré Město 🅼 Náměstí Republiky 🍽 Rybí trh (p78)

Hotel U Tří Pštrosů (4, A3)

At the end of Charles Bridge, this stately old inn, whose odd name (At the Three Ostriches) comes from a legend that some foreign visitors stayed here bringing ostriches as a gift for Emperor Charles IV. Rooms are elegantly furnished but small, and you'll pay more for a bridge view.

☎ 257 288 888 🖳 www .utripstrosu.cz ✉ Dražického náměstí 12, Malá Strana 🅼 Malostranská 🍽

Old Town Square Hotel (7, D2)

This chic hotel occupies a Unesco World Heritage–listed 16th-century townhouse slap bang in the middle of Old Town Square. Large contemporary style rooms feature black-and-white minimalism and Philippe Starck bathrooms with heated floors. Double-glazing eliminates most of the noise from the square.

☎ 221 421 111 🖳 www .otsh.com ✉ Staroměstské náměstí 20, Staré Město 🅼 Staroměstská 🍽 Ambiente Ristorante Pasta Fresca (p74)

MIDRANGE

Botel Admirál (6, C5)

Step aboard the Admiral, a permanently berthed ship on the west bank of the Vltava, for an unusual sleeping option. Spruced-up cabins are small but cosy, and those facing the river have admirable views. The 'botel' has a restaurant and nightclub.

☎ 257 321 302 🖳 www .admiral-botel.cz ✉ Hořejší nábřeží 57, Smíchov 🅼 Anděl 🍽

Castle Steps Hotel (5, B3)

Superb value rooms and suites spread over three separate but neighbouring 16th-century buildings, and all within walking distance of Prague Castle. Full of history and character, this is a friendly place, and as rooms come in different sizes and shapes, you may want to look over a few first.

☎ 257 531 941 🖳 www .pragueroom.com ✉ Nerudova 10, Malá Strana 🅼 Malostranská 🍽 Square (p71)

Hotel Betlem Club (4, C4-D4)

This historic old building, commanding the southern flank of Betlémské náměstí, dates back to the 13th century, and in its time has been a wedding gift, a brothel and a funeral parlour. Today it's a peaceful, stylish little hotel with a choice of rooms, such as cheaper, and slightly smaller, attic rooms.

☎ 222 221 574 🖳 www .betlemclub.cz ✉ Betlém-

Eclectic collection of rooftops border Old Town Square

ské náměstí 9, Staré Město
Ⓜ Můstek ⊠ Klub
Architektů (p76)

Hotel Clementin (7, B3)
In the heart of the Old
Town, the Clementin is a
newly refurbished hotel,
located in a strikingly slim
townhouse – allegedly the
narrowest in Prague – dating
back to 1360. There are just
nine smallish rooms, all with
the expected mod cons and
smart modern bathrooms.
☎ 222 221 798
🖥 www.clementin.cz
⊠ Seminářská 4, Staré
Město Ⓜ Staroměstská
⊠ Reykjavík (p77)

Hotel Da Vinci (6, D5)
This smart, and rather pink,
modern hotel, opened in
2005, has stylish rooms in
a tasteful black-and-white
décor scheme, with large,
gleaming bathrooms. Prints
of Leonardo's artworks adorn
the public areas. Not in the
prettiest surrounds, but it's
very close to the metro.
☎ 234 708 690 🖥 www
.hoteldavinci.cz ⊠ Na
Bojišti 28, Nové Město Ⓜ IP
Pavlova ⊠ Peking (p73)

Hotel U Klenotníka
(4, D4)
Located roughly halfway
between Old Town
Square and Wenceslas
Square, this neat little hotel
has just ten simply furnished
rooms. Public areas are
styled with a bit more flair,
and the front windows
are full of local artworks
for sale.
☎ 224 211 699 🖥 www
.uklenotnika.cz ⊠ Rytířská
3, Staré Město Ⓜ Můstek
⊠ Made in Japan (p76)

Flying the flag at Ametyst (p99)

Hotel U Tří Bubnů (7, C2)
'At The Three Drums' is a
unique place, on the corner
of Old Town Square, made
up of two tall, skinny
medieval houses. Wooden-
beam ceilings, brick arches
and stone vaults add to the
historic character, while
rooms are spacious, stylishly
furnished and fitted with
TVs and minibars. Bathrooms
are tiny.
☎ 224 214 855
🖥 www.utribubnu.cz
⊠ U radnice 8, Staré
Město Ⓜ Staroměstská
⊠ Jáchymka (p76)

Můstek Hotel (4, E4)
Standing on one of Prague's
busiest pedestrian thor-
oughfares near Wenceslas
Square, this discreet hotel
has 13 rooms, all differently
styled and priced, some with
original painted wooden-
beam ceilings, others with

bright orange walls. Take
your pick!
☎ 224 228 511 🖥 www
.mustekhotel.com ⊠ Na
můstku 3, Staré Město
Ⓜ Můstek ⊠ Made in
Japan (p76)

Pension U Červené Židle
(4, C4)
The new 'Red Chair' offers
simple yet stylish rooms in a
renovated townhouse just off
Betlémské' náměstí. Décor is
contemporary and unfussy,
and all rooms have minibar,
modem, TV and a bright
bathroom. The price is good
for the location.
☎ 296 180 018
🖥 www.redchairpension
.com ⊠ Liliová 4, Staré
Město Ⓜ Národní Třída
⊠ V Zátiší (p78)

Sieber Hotel (6, E4)
The Sieber is an attractive
four-star hotel occupying a

CATERING FOR KIDS

Most places can provide child-sized cots or beds, and most of those with on-site restaurants can handle the concept of smaller portions. Facilities for kids to amuse themselves, however, are almost exclusively found in top-end places, and usually come in the form of the odd board game and video distraction. Deluxe and top-end places generally have child-minding services.

If it's any consolation, lots of places will put kids under six or seven years of age up for the night for free – check what arrangements may apply when you book.

recently restored 19th-century townhouse in a quiet part of Vinohrady. Rooms are elegantly decorated in neutral tones, and there's a very good restaurant attached. Breakfast is 350Kč extra.
☎ 224 250 025 ☐ www .sieber.cz ✉ Slezská 55, Vinohrady Ⓜ Jiřího z Poděbra ✖ Los v Oslu (p79)

BUDGET

A-Plus Hotel & Hostel (4, H2)
The clean, simple rooms at A Plus have between one and 14 beds; some are en suite. There are also 'suites' with kitchenettes. There's a cheap restaurant on-site, and shared kitchens on each floor.
☎ 222 314 272 ☐ www .aplus-hostel.cz ✉ Na Florenci 1413, Nové Město Ⓜ Florenc ✖ Ⓥ

Clown & Bard Hostel (6, E4)
One of Prague's most popular hostels, offering simple but spotless doubles, dorms (four to six beds) and six-bed flats with kitchens. The lively cellar bar hosts regular guest-DJ nights and movies.
☎ 222 716 453 ☐ www .clownandbard.com

✉ Bořivojova 102, Žižkov Ⓜ Jiříhoz Poděbrad ✖

Hostel Týn (7, D1)
Cheap place offering dorms and doubles in a very central location, hidden away in a courtyard just off Old Town Square. A bargain if you want to be in the heart of things; predictably, it books up quickly.
☎ 224 828 519 ☐ http:// tyn.prague-hostels.cz ✉ Týnská 19, Staré Město Ⓜ Náměstí Republiky ✖ Beas (p75)

Hostel U Melounu (6, D5)
One of Prague's prettiest budget options, the ground level of 'At the Watermelon' has singles, twins, dorms and apartments (some with en suites) arranged around a lovely garden with a barbecue. Discounts offered for longer stays.
☎ 224 916 322 ☐ www .hostelumelounu.cz ✉ Ke Karlovu 7, Nové Město Ⓜ IP Pavlova

Hotel Imperial (4, G2)
The deep, dark corridors and air of bygone intrigue that hovers over the Imperial provide an atmospheric glimpse of old Prague. The very simple rooms, and the communal showers and toilets could

do with a thorough overhaul, but this is still amazing value.
☎ 222 316 012 ☐ www .hotelimperial.cz ✉ Na Poříčí 15, Nové Město Ⓜ Náměstí Republiky ✖ Kavárna Imperial (p73)

Ritchie's Hostel (7, B3)
In the middle of the Old Town, Ritchie's offers clean dorms and doubles above a row of souvenir shops, on a very busy street. There's a bar, a lounge and Internet access for guests, and breakfast is 75Kč extra.
☎ 222 221 229 ☐ www .ritchieshostel.cz ✉ Karlova 9, Staré Město Ⓜ Staroměstská

Travellers' Hostel Island (4, B6)
The most attractively located of Prague's five 'Travellers' Hostels', this sociable backpacker place has huge dorms with between 20 and 50 beds, though it's only open May to September. There's a café, a pub and Internet access, and an open-air cinema on the island.
☎ 224 932 991 ☐ www .travellers.cz ✉ Střelecký Ostrov, Malá Strana Ⓜ Národní Třída, then tram 6, 9, 22, 23, 57 or 58 to most Legií ✖

About Prague

Prague's multifarious charms are certainly no secret. Visitors have been flocking here since the end of the old totalitarian regime to absorb the magnificent architectural legacies of castles and churches, and the cultural treasures of its museums and galleries. Prague's seemingly endless popularity with international tourists does of course mean crowds, queues and the steady growth of less savoury attractions like the tacky strip clubs, casinos and bars catering to boozed-up stag parties. But once you walk away from the busy main thoroughfares, you can find yourself wandering along virtually deserted cobbled lanes and through beautiful little squares and leafy parks that look like elements from a period film set, and have probably been used as such.

Snemovni náměstí at night

The locals can sometimes seem famously indifferent, but often this is just a tourist-weary façade or an indigenous bluntness. Don't be fooled into thinking that a gruff noise is the start and end of communication. Try a few words of broken Czech, and see what happens. Not bad as a motto for your stay in Prague, really.

HISTORY
In the Beginning

Farming communities settled around Prague as far back as 4000 BC. The region was then occupied by a Celtic tribe known as the Boii, who gave their name to 'Bohemia'. Germanic tribes later moved into the area, and in the 6th century, two Slav tribes, the Czechs and the Zličani, settled on either side of the Vltava.

The Czech Přemysl dynasty, under Prince Bořivoj, established Prague Castle in the 870s and Christianity was adopted during the rule of 'Good King Wenceslas' from 925 to 935, but in 950 Bohemia was engulfed by the Holy Roman Empire. Prague prospered under the rule of Emperor Charles IV (1346–78), whose Gothic handiwork is still to be seen everywhere, from the eponymous Charles Bridge and Charles University to St Vitus Cathedral.

Church reform became a hot topic in the late 14th and early 15th centuries. Jan Hus led a vocal reform movement (Hussitism) and was subsequently burned at the stake in 1415, provoking a rebellion that eventually put the Hussites in charge; their king from 1452 to 1471 was George of Poděbrady. The Czech nobility arranged for the Austrian Catholic Habsburgs to rule in 1526. Prague became the Habsburg seat, and enjoyed a brief 'Golden Age' as capital of the Holy Roman Empire under the rule of the eccentric Rudolf II. But an uprising in 1618 resulted in the Thirty Years' War, the death of a quarter of the region's population, and ultimately the loss of Czech independence for 300 years.

Czech National Revival

Literature, journalism, architecture and drama flourished in Prague during the 19th-century Czech National Revival. One attempt to reclaim Czech identity was historian František Palacký's seminal *Dějiny národu Českého* (History of the Czech Nation). In 1861 the Czechs finally wrested control of Prague in council elections, but the country remained under Austrian rule. The National Theatre, National Museum and Municipal House were all products of the growing sense of national identity.

Independence & War

The Czechs had no enthusiasm for fighting for the decaying Austro-Hungarian Empire during WWI, and there were international pleas from Czechs and Slovaks for independence. Finally, on 28 October 1918, Czechoslovakia was born. Its capital was Prague, and its first leader the popular Tomáš Masaryk.

In 1938 the Nazis marched into the largely German-speaking Sudetenland, and in 1939 they occupied Bohemia and Moravia too. By the time WWII concluded, the Nazis had devastated nearly all of Prague's

Garden havens are scattered throughout Prague

120,000-strong Jewish population. One of the newly reinstated government's first acts was to expel Sudeten Germans, and thousands perished on the forced marches to Bavaria and Austria.

Communism

The Communist Party won over a third of the Czechoslovakian popular vote in the 1946 elections and formed a coalition government with other socialist parties. But after intense bickering with local democrats, the communists seized control, with the Soviet Union's support, in 1948. The next decade and a half saw economic policies that brought Czechoslovakia close

A WORD OF HURT

Czechs are responsible for the introduction of a rather unpleasant word to the English language. The word is 'defenestration', which means 'the act of throwing a thing or especially a person out of a window'. It was coined in 1419 when Hussites, still angry about the execution of their figurehead four years earlier, threw several Catholic councillors out of an upper window of Prague's New Town Hall. The incident was reprised with devastating consequences in 1618 when a couple of Habsburg councillors exited Prague Castle in similar fashion, sparking off the Thirty Years' War.

to financial ruin, and an intolerance of political rivals, which led to widespread persecution. Thousands of people, including top party members, died in labour camps, or were executed outright, and many fled the country.

Prague Spring & Charter 77

In the late 1960s, national Communist Party leader Alexander Dubček showed reformist colours through rapid liberalisation under the banner of 'socialism with a human face' and there was a cultural resurgence in literature, theatre and film, led by such luminaries as Milan Kundera, Bohumil Hrabel, Václav Havel and Miloš Forman. The Soviet regime crushed this 'Prague Spring' on the night of 20 August 1968, with Warsaw Pact military hardware, and Dubček was replaced by the orthodox Gustáv Husák. In January 1977 a document called Charta 77 (Charter 77) was signed by 243 intellectuals and artists, including Václav Havel. This public demand for basic human rights became an anticommunist tenet for dissidents.

National Velvet

A violent attack by police on hundreds of people attending a rally in Prague on 17 November 1989 generated continuous public demonstrations, culminating in 750,000 people gathering on Letná plain. A group led by Havel procured the government's resignation on 3 December, and 26 days later he was the new leader. This period of nonviolent demonstration became known as the 'Velvet Revolution'. Peaceful 'problem-solving' was repeated when Slovak and Czech leaders agreed to go their separate ways on 1 January 1993, the day Prague became capital of the new Czech Republic and Havel its president.

New Independence

Subsequent years were marred by financial scandals and a highly un-popular, and unstable, power-sharing arrangement between the two main parties, the left-wing Social Democrats (ČSSD) and the conservative Civic Democratic Party (ODS). Havel barely weathered the 1998 presidential elections, scraping in by a margin of just one vote, and stepped down in 2003 as Václav Klaus took over the reins.

In 1999 the Czech Republic joined NATO and in 2004 it became a member of the EU. Unemployment remains a problem, but the continuing influx of tourists has given a huge boost to the whole Czech economy.

ENVIRONMENT

Traffic snarls are a major source of noxious irritation for anyone out for a walk in the late afternoon, particularly anywhere on the main roads around the centre. This, however, is nothing compared to the fume-laden haze that settles during the occasional winter inversions.

The Vltava has a less-than-pristine reputation when it comes to water quality, no thanks to the industrial pollution of the past, and the increasing traffic plying the water in the name of tourism. But some fearless (or brainless) people have been spotted taking morning dips off Slovanský ostrov, and early evening on the riverbank off Josefov often finds someone with a line in the water.

Recycling is deeply imprinted on Czech domestic life, with large bins, in prominent locations, accepting paper, plastics and glassware; most glass beer bottles can be recycled at supermarkets in return for a refundable deposit. If you're staying near any main thoroughfare in the Old Town, you can expect some noise pollution from late-night drunks.

Prague suffered its worst flood in centuries in August 2002, with large parts of the city underwater and the metro system inoperable for months afterwards. Some of the sorriest scenes were at the zoo, which was decimated and many animals killed. The clean-up continued until well into 2003, though Prague has since made a healthy comeback.

Lights reflect on Vltava River at Smetanova Embankment

GOVERNMENT & POLITICS

Prague is the capital of the Czech Republic, a parliamentary democracy with a president (currently Václav Klaus) chosen by parliament for a five-year term. The president, in turn, chooses the prime minister, who, along with the cabinet (*vláda*), holds the real decision-making power. The parliament has a House of Representatives (*poslanecká sněmovna*) and a Senate (*sénat*), both publicly elected.

DID YOU KNOW?
- Population 1.2 million
- Inflation 2%
- Unemployment around 9%
- Average monthly wage 29,000Kč
- Average price of pub beer 25Kč per 500mL

Prague's governing body, the Local Government of the Capital City of Prague, has its seat elsewhere and is represented by a municipal office acting in concert with a mayor-headed council. The city contains 10 districts and 57 suburbs, each with their own district and local governments.

The Prague electorate has lately favoured the right-leaning ODS, in contrast to a national trend supporting the left-leaning ČSSD, whose leader is the current prime minister, Jiří Paroubek. The Communist Party still has a dedicated core (albeit an elderly one) of supporters.

Although the people of Prague voted overwhelmingly in favour of EU membership, the turnout for subsequent elections to the European Parliament was low, and enthusiasm for the international body seems to be thin on the ground.

ECONOMY

After plunging into recession in the late 1990s, the Czech economy has been more robust in recent years, and grew by 4% in 2004. Accession to the EU in that year brought financial benefits and responsibilities, and gave impetus to much-needed reforms, but unemployment has continued to rise, and currently stands at around 9%. The majority of Prague's population is employed in one of the service industries, and a large proportion of those are connected in some way to the ever-growing local tourist industry. The swelling number of visitors to Prague contributes enormously to the local economy and obviously has a flow-on effect impacting the entire Czech Republic.

Roughly 10% of the population is employed in the manufacturing industry, specifically textiles, food and machinery. These activities take place mainly in the industrial suburbs of Smíchov and Karlín.

SOCIETY & CULTURE

Czechs have a west Slavic background. The two main minority groups in Prague are Roma (also known as gypsies) and Slovaks. There are also several sizable expat communities living and working in Prague, mainly contingents of Americans, Germans and Ukrainians, and a growing number of British and Irish; it's thought they make up about 4% to 5% of the city's total population.

> ### ROMA
> Roma (*romové* or *cikáni;* also known as Gypsies) are a minority group (0.3%) with a line-age that extends back to 15th-century India. They suffer neglect and hostility across the Czech Republic and Central Europe, due to a lack of acceptance of their generally closed, transient lifestyle; Roma involvement in petty theft and fraud in lieu of the unskilled work they are normally restricted to; and, unfortunately, flat-out racism.
>   The lack of Czech action to address the Roma's disproportionate levels of poverty, illiteracy and unemployment has been criticised by the EU.

Czechs tend to be restrained socially, though they often let their hair down in the more popular beer halls, or nontourist bars or restaurants. They have a dry and sardonic sense of humour, not too dissimilar to the British, though of course if you don't understand the language, you just won't get it. Generally, the people of Prague are mild-mannered and polite – the few exceptions include fanatical football fans and some of the more jaded staff at touristy pubs and restaurants. On a serious note, there have occasionally been reports of muggings, and attacks by skinheads on dark-skinned people.

Some common Czech civilities, which are also appreciated when uttered by visitors, include: *dobrý den* (good morning); *dobrý večer* (good evening); *prosím* (please); *na shledanou* (goodbye) and *nazdravi* (cheers).

Etiquette
Czechs don't stand on ceremony, and when attending most shows around town, you can wear pretty much anything you want. If you're going to the opera, ballet or a concert at the larger or more traditional venues, however, smart casual is the preferred style. Except at upmarket private functions, black tie will look out of place, as will the tourist uniform of baseball cap and shorts.

Smoking is common and there are few places that restrict or ban the activity, with obvious exceptions being inside public transport, museums, galleries and the like. It's the custom in many eateries to resist smoking over lunch, even if there are ashtrays on the table – if in doubt, ask a waiter.

ARTS
Architecture
The earliest architectural style that graces Prague is Romanesque (10th to 12th centuries), featuring heavy stone walls with small windows; fine examples include the Basilica of St George and the Old Town Hall cellar. Gothic architecture (13th to 16th centuries), built around ribbed vaults with high pointed arches, is exemplified by St Vitus' façade and the spindly heights of Týn Church. Renaissance architecture (15th to 17th centuries) is classical, symmetrical, and often decorated with *sgraffito* (a multilayered mural technique), as at the Ball-Game House in the Royal

Garden. Flamboyant baroque (17th to 18th centuries) is on display in profusion across the city, with St Nicholas Church in Malá Strana being perhaps the best example. Late baroque evolved into an even more florid style called rococo, as seen in the façade of the Kinský Palace.

The revivalist period (late 18th to 19th centuries) made the city like old, with resurrected styles applied to buildings including the neo-Renaissance National Theatre, while colourful Art Nouveau (c 1899–1912) produced numerous splendid structures such as the Municipal House. Between 1910 and 1920, cubism was applied to unique buildings such as the House of the Black Madonna, after which Art Deco, plain old functionalism and fantastically ugly communist residential blocks found their place in the city. The mixed styles post-1989 are hard to quantify but can be brilliantly original, such as in the form of the Dancing Building.

Painting

The Czech lands have produced prodigious artists for at least 600 years. Magister Theodoricus' painting impressed other Central European artists in the 14th century and can be seen in St Vitus' Chapel of St Wenceslas. Realism and romanticism were popular in the 19th century, with Mikuláš Aleš and the prolific Mánes family leading the charge; father Antonín was known for landscapes, son Josef for portraits and rural views, and other son Quido for quirky and sentimental 'genre scenes' of everyday life.

Art Nouveau's patron saint was Alfons Mucha, whose works are shown at the Mucha Museum. Famous impressionists of the same period included Max Švabinský and Antonín Slavíček. In the 20th century, cubist artists such as Emil Fila and Josef Čapek, and symbolists like František Kupka made way for the surrealism of František Janoušek and later the socialist realism of Joseph Brož.

KAFKAESQUE

Even in his most lurid dreams, Franz Kafka could never have anticipated, or desired, his elevation to his modern status of lucrative municipal icon. Posters, T-shirts, mugs and other touristy paraphernalia carrying the writer's image fill souvenir shops across Prague, and, of course, his books have been translated into several languages. Aside from the Franz Kafka Museum (4, B3; p26) in Malá Strana, numerous places either advertise a personal connection or invent an association. Places that were personally occupied by Kafka's unique brand of paranoia include his birthplace (7, C2), which is on the edge of Old Town Square and now houses a rather lacklustre exhibition; Dum U minuty (7, C2-C3), where he lived from 1889 to 1896; the Little Blue Cottage (8, E1) in Golden Lane, where he lived from 1916 to 1917; and the oppressive insurance office (4, G2-G3), now the Mercure Hotel, where he worked from 1908 to 1922.

The last few decades have seen artists making grotesquery brush strokes (Jiří Načeradský) and fusing with electronic media (Woody Vašulka). The work of most of these artists is displayed at the Centre For Modern & Contemporary Art in Holešovice.

Literature

František Palacký's voluminous history of Bohemia and Moravia, the poems of Karel Hynek Mácha, the short stories of Jan Neruda and the romanticism of Božena Němcová were some of Czech literature's 19th-century standouts. Czechoslovakia's first leader, Tomáš Masaryk, was also an accomplished author and philosopher.

At the start of the 20th century, Franz Kafka, writing in German, expressed his claustrophobic fears in *The Castle*, while contemporary author Jaroslav Hašek wrote in Czech, and in a considerably lighter vein, about the knockabout antics of a Czech army conscript in *The Good Soldier Švejk*. Karel Čapek gave robots to science fiction in *RUR* (Rossum's Universal Robots), and poet Jaroslav Seiffert's efforts pre-WWII eventually led to the Nobel Prize for Literature in 1984. Milan Kundera's books are internationally known, as is the work of Ivan Klima, who wrote *The Ship Named Hope* and an excellent collection of essays, *The Spirit of Prague*. Bohumil Hrabal's *The Little Town That Stood Still* is another international hit.

Music

Prague has a rich and varied musical tradition. Its most illustrious visitor was Mozart, who conducted the premiere of his opera *Don Giovanni* here and dedicated one of his symphonies to the city. The mid-19th century saw a crop of great composers emerging, including Bedřich Smetana (1824–84) and Antonín Dvořák (1841–1904), best known for his symphony, *From the New World*.

Immortalised Antonín Dvořák

Prague has a deep-rooted jazz scene, with Czechs figuring prominently in European jazz circles until the 1948 communist coup d'état. The 1960s brought a less censorial atmosphere and the appearance of Prague's first professional jazz club, Reduta (p88). Rock and pop remained largely underground movements before the changes of 1989. The top Czech band of the '70s was Plastic People of the Universe, whose members achieved international fame after being imprisoned for their 'subversive' sounds. In recent years, everything from hard rock to country and western has taken off, and leading contemporary performers include grunge band Support Lesbiens and violinist Iva Bittová.

ARRIVAL & DEPARTURE
Air
Praha Ruzyně airport (6, A3; www.csl .cz/en/) is about 20km west of the city centre, and accessible by a combination of bus and metro. The main building shelters an arrival hall and a departure hall. Facilities include a bar, fast-food outlets, Internet access, travel and accommodation agencies, and a scattering of ATMs and money-exchange offices.

INFORMATION
Car Park Information (☎ 220 113 408)
General Inquiries (☎ 220 113 314)

HOTEL BOOKING SERVICE
AVE (☎ 220 114 650)
Čedok (☎ 220 113 744)

FLIGHT INFORMATION
Air France (☎ 221 113 737)
British Airways (☎ 239 000 299)
ČSA (☎ 239 007 007)
KLM (☎ 233 090 933)
Lufthansa (☎ 220 114 456)

AIRPORT ACCESS
Public transport information is available from the airport office in the city transport department, **Dopravní podnik** (DP; ☎ 296 191 817; www.dpp.cz).

Bus & Metro
From in front of the airport's main building, catch bus 119 or 254 to Dejvická metro station, then ride line A into the centre; the trip takes about 45 minutes. Alternatively, buses 179 and 225 run to Nové Butovice metro station in Prague's southwest, from where line B heads into town.

Bus & Tram
Between midnight and 3.30am, catch night bus 510 and transfer to city-bound tram 51 at Divoká Šárká stop.

Minibus
Vans operated by **Cedaz** (☎ 220 114 296) run between the airport and náměstí Republiky for 90Kč per person. The vehicles can also be commissioned to drive from the airport to anywhere in the centre for 480Kč for up to four people (960Kč for five to eight people). Cedaz operates from the airport between 6am and 9pm, and from náměstí Republiky between 5.30am and 9.30pm.

Taxi
There's a desk in the Arrivals Hall for **Airport Cars** (☎ 220 113 892; ☺ 8am-11pm); no other taxis can stop outside the Arrivals Hall. A trip into the city will cost upwards of 650Kč per person depending on destintion. From Old Town Square in a regular taxi, you'll pay around 500Kč to the airport.

Bus
The state-owned bus company, **Czech Automobile Transport** (ČSAD; ☎ 900 144 444 premium-rate 14Kč per min; www.jizd nirady.cz), operates regional and long-distance domestic coaches from Florenc bus station (4, J3). Information is available in Florenc's central hall at **window 8** (☺ 6am-9pm), online or by phone.

A number of international coaches service Prague, including a Czech line handled by **Bohemia Euroexpress International** (4, J2; ☎ 224 814 450; 🖳 www.bei.cz; Křižikova 4-6) near Florenc bus station, and those belonging to the Eurolines consortium, whose main Prague agent is **Sodeli CZ** (4, G4; ☎ 224 239 318; Senovážné náměstí 6). Most coaches operate from stands at Florenc bus station, and from one at Nádraží Holešovice metro station.

Train
Inexpensive and reliable domestic services are provided by **Czech Railways** (ČD; ☎ 221 111 122; www.cd.cz). You can buy plain tickets *(jízdenka)* or tickets with a reservation *(místenka)* for a seat, couchette or sleeper; when scanning timetables, look out for services designated 'R' (reservations recommended) or a circled/boxed 'R' (reservations mandatory).

Most international trains arriving in Prague pull up at the multilevel main train station, **Praha Hlavní Nádraží** (4, H5; ☎ 224 641 881), though some end up at stations at Smíchov (6, B5) and Holešovice (4, C2).

Travel Documents
PASSPORT
Those requiring a visa to visit the Czech Republic must have a passport valid for at least three months longer than the validity of the visa.

VISA
EU citizens, plus citizens of Norway, Switzerland and Iceland, can stay in the Czech Republic indefinitely and without the need of a visa. Citizens of Australia, New Zealand, the USA and Canada can visit visa-free for up to 90 days.

RETURN/ONWARD TICKET
A return or onward ticket is usually (but for some reason not always) required to gain entry to the Czech Republic.

Customs & Duty Free
Visitors can import or export unlimited amounts of foreign currency, and up to 350,000Kč in Czech currency. Higher amounts must be declared to Customs.

You can import 2L of wine, 1L of spirits and 200 cigarettes without paying duty, as well as gifts (noncommercial goods) collectively worth under 6000Kč; quantities of these goods over the specified limits have to be declared on arrival. Treat that potential genuine antique buy of a lifetime with caution, as the real deal cannot be exported. When on a shopping spree, remember that purchases exceeding 30,000Kč attract a 22% duty.

Left Luggage
There is a 24-hour left-luggage service in the arrival hall that charges 40Kč per piece of luggage.

GETTING AROUND
Prague's cheap, extensive and relatively easy public transport system is run by its transport department, **Dopravní podnik** (☎ 296 191 817; www.dpp.cz), which maintains information centres at the airport and in four metro stations, including **Muzeum** (4, G6; ⊙ 7am-9pm), **Můstek** (4, F5; ⊙ 7am-6pm Mon-Fri) and **Anděl** (6, B5; ⊙ 7am-6pm Mon-Fri). Most visitors rely on the underground metro to sweep them from one side of the city to the other. Trams are also convenient, with 26 daytime routes and a handful of night-time services negotiating all the main inner city areas. Buses are mostly useful for filling in the urban gaps in the metro and tram systems, as they cover pretty much everywhere beyond the centre. Pick up the detailed *Prague Transport* or the simpler *Through Prague Quickly and Easily with Us* pamphlets from an information office.

Single transfer tickets (20/10Kč) are good for all public transport for 75 minutes from the moment you punch them into a validation machine (for 1½ hours 8pm to 5am Monday to Friday and all day Saturday and Sunday). Single nontransfer tickets (14/7Kč) are for short hops lasting no more than 20 minutes on buses and trams, or up to four metro stations; they are not valid for the funicular or for night transport. Tickets can be bought from ticket machines in the metro stations and at newsstands, various hotels and travel agencies. Make sure you validate your ticket before entering the 'ticket compulsory area' of metro stations. or upon boarding buses or trams. Spot inspections are frequent and unwitting tourists are favourite targets. Inspectors' salaries are partly based on the number of fines they hand out, so they're keen to catch you!

Travel Passes
Most short-stay visitors will find it cost effective to buy tickets as they need them. If you anticipate jumping on and off public transport more than a few times per

day, you should buy a short-term season pass, allowing unlimited use of the metro, trams, buses and the Petřín funicular for one, three, seven or 15 days at a cost of 80/220/280/320Kč. Longer-term passes, valid for between one month and a year are also available. You need to show valid ID to purchase these. Don't forget to validate these passes the first time you use them.

Car

On a short trip to Prague, you're unlikely to need your own wheels, and the narrow, cobblestone streets of the historic district and the newer roads choked with trams, cars and human traffic don't make driving a pleasure. If you do need to drive, however, there are a number of rental agencies with offices at the airport.

Avis (☎ 810 777 810; www.avis.cz) From around €75 per day.

Budget (☎ 220 113 253; www.budget.cz) From around €76 per day.

Czechocar CS (☎ 220 113 454; www.cze chocar.cz) From 1600Kč per day.

Hertz (☎ 233 326 714; www.hertz.cz) From 2480Kč per day.

Metro

The swift 51-station metro operates from 5am until midnight, and comprises three lines, each identified by a letter and colour: A (green), B (yellow) and C (red). To leave a station, head for a sign saying *výstup* (exit); for a connecting line, look for a *přestup*. Disabled travellers should note that the barrier-free access to platforms is more a feature of suburban metro stations than inner city ones, the exceptions being Muzeum, Vyšehrad and Hlavní Nádraží.

Taxi

Unfortunately Prague has an oversupply of crooked taxi drivers who do a major disservice to the honest ones. It is illegal for taxis to stop for fares anywhere other than at a designated rank, so don't flag down a cab, or use a taxi rank in any of the main tourist areas, unless you want to be grossly overcharged. It's far better to call one of the following, usually reliable, 24-hour radio taxis:

AAA Radio Taxi (☎ 140 14)
City Taxi (☎ 257 257 257)
Halo Taxi (☎ 244 114 411)
Profi Taxi (☎ 261 314 151)

Tram & Bus

The numbers allocated to tram lines have one to two digits, while bus route numbers have three digits. During the 'day', trams and buses run from 4.30am until 12.15am, with more limited, but still fairly regular, 'night' services in the intervening time; night-time routes are serviced by buses numbered 501 to 512 and trams numbered 51 to 59. The info centres in Muzeum, Můstek, Anděl, Černý Most and Nádraží Holešovice metro stations supply timetables and route maps for the tram and bus systems.

PRACTICALITIES
Business Hours

The following hours are just a rough guide, and can fluctuate wildly according to the type of business, season and location; note that tourist-oriented places are generally open longer hours and often on Sunday.

Attractions (10am-6pm; many museums and galleries close Mon)
Offices (9am-5pm Mon-Fri)
Post offices (8am-6pm Mon-Fri, 8am-noon Sat)
Restaurants (11am-11pm)
Shops (9am-6pm Mon-Fri, 10am-1pm Sat)

Climate & When to Go

Prague is popular year-round, but tourists are especially numerous from May to June and over Easter, Christmas and New Year's, when getting across Charles Bridge becomes impossible without a catapult. May and September, the months on either side of the hot, downpour-prone summer, usually have the best weather for exploring the city. Though the snowy winters get very cold and are susceptible to smog alerts, it can be a beautiful time to visit and accommodation is plentiful. From the beginning of the low season in October, many attractions and businesses start limiting their hours, or close until the following summer.

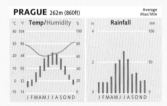

Disabled Travellers

Prague is making an effort to address the needs of disabled travellers, though in some areas facilities are still sorely lacking. Wheelchair-accessible public transport is limited to several train and metro stations with self-operating lifts, plus special buses plying two routes on weekdays linking destinations such as Hradčanská, Florenc and Náměstí Republiky. There are two dozen suburban lines serviced by low-platform buses. Pedestrian-crossing lights in the centre make a ticking noise to indicate a green light to the visually impaired, and some museums now have tactile displays and Braille text. More performance venues are equipped with wheelchair access, and some have good facilities for the hearing impaired. The 'limited', 'good' and 'excellent' disabled access ratings given to tourist sites in this book reflect the relative ease with which those in wheelchairs can reasonably visit these places. Museums and galleries often have ramps and/or lifts, enabling access to at least some of their collections. Older structures are prohibited in some cases from making such alterations to their structural fabric. Cobblestone roads may also prove difficult.

INFORMATION & ORGANISATIONS

A comprehensive source of information for wheelchair-bound travellers is the **Prague**

Wheelchair Users Organisation (Pražská organizace vozíčkářů; 4, F2; ☎ 224 827 210; www.pov.cz; Benediktská 6, Josefov). It produces the booklet *Barrier-Free Prague,* listing accessible venues, reserved parking places, transport options and tours of historical areas. The Czech-language monthly *Přehled* also lists wheelchair-friendly venues.

The **Union of the Blind & Weak Sighted** (Sjednocená organizace nevidomých a slabozrakých v Čr; 4, F6; ☎ 221 462 146; Krakovská 21) can provide information to the vision-impaired. There are useful links at www.braillnet.cz (in Czech).

Discounts

Students, children under 15, and families get discounts at most tourist attractions and on public transport. Some venues offer reductions, but many just have different levels of fixed-price seating. To qualify for local concession cards seniors need to be Czech citizens; the same applies to disabled travellers. That said, a number of places will grant concessions regardless of the formalities, and others will only have a cursory glance at the card you're waving at them.

The Prague Card offers three days of free access to many museums and galleries. It's available from official tourist offices, **Čedok** (7, F3; Na příkopě 18), and several other travel agencies, and costs 590/410Kč. It no longer incorporates a travel pass; this must be purchased separately (see p112).

YOUTH CARDS

Bring an international student identity card (ISIC). Youth cards such as Euro26 and Go25 will also get you discounts at many museums, theatres and galleries, plus some hostels.

Electricity

Cycle AC
Frequency 50Hz
Plugs two round pins
Voltage 220V

Embassies & Consulates

Australia (4, F2; ☎ 296 578 350; Unit 6/3, Solitaire Office Building, Klimentská 10, Praha 1)

Canada (6, C2-B3; ☎ 272 101 800; Muchova 6, Praha 6)

France (4, A4; ☎ 251 171 711; Velkopřerovské náměstí 2, Malá Strana)

Germany (5, A4; ☎ 257 113 111; Vlašská 19, Praha 1)

Ireland (5, C4; ☎ 257 530 061; Tržiště 13, Malá Strana)

New Zealand (6, E5; ☎ 222 514 672; Dykova 19, Praha 1)

South Africa (6, E5; ☎ 267 311 114; Ruská 65, Vršovice)

UK (5, C3; ☎ 257 402 111; Thunovská 14, Praha 1)

USA (5, B4; ☎ 257 530 663; Tržiště 15, Praha 1)

Emergencies

Pickpocketing is an increasing problem in places where tourists congregate, so do watch your belongings at all times, don't leave anything unattended anywhere, and don't leave bags or cameras dangling over one shoulder. Muggings have also occurred in metro stations. One recent scam has involved that old favourite, black market money changing, with gullible tourists handing over their cash and receiving a wad of worthless Bulgarian banknotes in exchange, apparently not noticing that they're printed in the Cyrillic alphabet for a start. Visitors have also been targeted by men posing as police – one version of this scam involves the 'cops' asking to see the foreigner's money and then returning it minus a few notes (or just bolting off with the lot). The police do not have the power to search you in this manner, and if you doubt the authenticity of an official who approaches you, hang on to your wallet and passport and insist on going with them to the nearest police station. To make a police report regarding stolen property, head to the interpreter-equipped **Praha 1 police station** (4, E5; ☎ 261 451 760; Jungmannovo náměstí 9). Genuine public transport inspectors will have to show you their badge when they approach you. If they fine you, always ask for a receipt.

Prague is safe to walk around at night if you apply common sense and stay aware of your surroundings. Prostitutes, usually exploited by organised crime gangs, target tourists in the Old Town and around Wenceslas Square after dark. Avoid the park in front of the main train station at night.

Ambulance ☎ 155
Fire ☎ 150
Police (municipal) ☎ 156
Police (national) ☎ 158
Road Assistance ☎ 1230

Fitness
GYMS

Sport Club (7, D4; ☎ 221 094 331; www .sportklubbudivadla.cz; Rytířská 22, Staré Město) The usual treadmills and exercise bikes, plus sauna, whirlpool and massage.

YMCA Sport Centrum (4, G3; ☎ 224 875 811; www.scymca.cz; Na poříčí 12, Nové Město) Well-equipped exercise centre with a pool, gym and solarium.

SQUASH

Esquo Squashcentrum (6, A4; ☎ 233 109 301; www.squashstrahov.cz; Vaníčkova 2b, Strahov) This squash centre offers a number of modern courts.

SWIMMING

Sportcentrum Hotel Čechie (6, F3; ☎ 266 194 100; U Sluncové 618, Karlín) Big hotel complex with a pool and sauna available for nonguests.

TENNIS

Ostrov Štvanice (6, D3; ☎ 224 810 272; Ostrov Štvanice, Holešovice) This island, north of Florenc metro, hosts the prestigious Štvanice tennis club and a popular skateboard park.

Gay & Lesbian Travellers

Homosexuality is legal in the Czech Republic and the age of consent is 15. The gay scene in Prague is thriving, with a number of clubs, bars, restaurants and hotels catering to the community, and a couple of gay lifestyle magazines available on newsstands in the city centre. It's a discreet scene, however, with the various venues scattered across town, and concentrations in Vinohrady and Žižkov. Several establishments tailor themselves to both gays and lesbians, but the majority are gay-oriented; only one place (Maler; see p95) reserves evenings for lesbians. Do note, however, that some clubs are little more than sleazy pick-up stations frequented by rent-boys, and may be unsafe for tourists; there have been reports of robberies, and worse, in recent years. Visiting gay couples may trigger uncomfortable reactions from some locals if they display affection in public; it remains an unfamiliar sight to many Czechs.

INFORMATION & ORGANISATIONS

Comprehensive information on gay life in the city, including reviews, is online at **Prague Gay Guide** (http://prague.gayguide.net), while www.gay.cz also has some reviews of nightspots. **Amigo** (www.amigo.cz) is a bimonthly gay publication with venue/event information and lots of classifieds.

Health
IMMUNISATIONS

It's not necessary to get any vaccinations prior to your trip to the Czech Republic.

PRECAUTIONS

Prague enjoys a good standard of public hygiene, though you may not think so if you taste the unpleasantly chlorinated, but nonetheless usually drinkable, tap water. A less innocuous health risk is posed by the exhaust emissions that can cloud the city in winter during periods of extremely stable weather (known in meteorological terms as inversions).

Like anywhere else, practise the usual precautions when it comes to safe sex; condoms are available at any of the many pharmacies *(lekárna)*.

INSURANCE & MEDICAL TREATMENT

Travel insurance is advisable to cover medical treatment you may need while in Prague. First-aid outside a hospital *(nemocnice)* and emergency treatment are provided to visitors, but unless you are an EU citizen covered under a reciprocal health-care arrangement, you will have to pay full price for treatment. All foreigners must pay for their own prescriptions.

MEDICAL SERVICES

Hospitals and clinics with 24-hour emergency departments:

Health Centre Prague (4, E6; ☎ 224 220 040, after hours 603 433 833; www.doctor-prague.cz; No 3, 2nd fl, Vodičkova 28, Nové Město, Praha 1)

Na Homolce (☎ 257 271 111, after hours 257 272 111; www.homolka.cz; Roentgenova 2, Motol, Praha 5)

Policlinic at Národní (4, C5; ☎ 222 075 120, 24hr emergencies 777 942 270; Národní třída 9, Staré Město, Praha 1)

DENTAL SERVICES

For emergency dental treatment, head to the 24-hour **Praha 1 clinic** (4, E5; ☎ 224 946 981; Palackého 5, Nové Město).

PHARMACIES

The following pharmacies are open 24 hours:

Lékárna Palackého Praha 1 clinic (4, E5; ☎ 224 946 982; Palackého 5, Nové Město, Praha 1)

Lékárna U sv Ludmily (3, A2; ☎ 222 519 731; Belgická 37, Vinohrady, Praha 2)

Holidays
New Year's Day 1 January
Easter Monday March/April
Labour Day 1 May

Liberation Day 8 May
SS Cyril & Methodius Day 5 July
Jan Hus Day 6 July
Czech Statehood Day 28 September
Independence Day 28 October
Struggle for Freedom & Democracy Day 17 November
'Generous Day', Christmas Eve 24 December
Christmas Day 25 December
St Stephen's Day 26 December

Internet

There are plenty of places to log on in Prague – very useful if your accommodation is not connected. However, nearly all top-end hotels have on-site facilities or data points in rooms. Internet-café connection speeds and charges can vary significantly, with the terminal-heavy places usually charging the lowest prices – usually around 1Kč per minute. Some also have data points for plugging in your laptop.

INTERNET SERVICE PROVIDERS

Major Internet service providers you can access in Prague include **AOL** (www.aol.com), **CompuServe** (www.compuserve.com) and **AT&T** (www.attbusiness.net). If you have an account with one of these, you can download a list of local dial-in numbers.

INTERNET CAFÉS

Internet Post (4, F5; ☎ 222 244 727; Václavské náměstí 37; ✆ 9am-10pm)
Internet Spika (4, G3; ☎ 224 211 521; Dlažděná 4; ✆ 8am-midnight)
Na Schůdkách (4, G2; ☎ 222 310 184; Zlatnicka 11; ✆ 11am-midnight)

USEFUL WEBSITES

LonelyPlanet.com (www.lonelyplanet.com) is an excellent resource and offers a speedy link to many of Prague's best websites. Others to try:
Czech Centrum (www.czech.cz)
Czech Tourist Authority (www.czech tourism.cz)

Prague Doing Business (www.doing business.cz)
Prague Experience (www.prague experience.com)
Prague Post (www.praguepost.com)
Prague TV (www.prague.tv)
Square Meal (www.squaremeal.cz)

Lost Property

Try the city's **lost-and-found office** (4, C5; ztráty a nálezy; ☎ 224 235 085; Karoliny Světlé 5). **Ruzyně airport** (☎ 220 114 283) has a 24-hour lost-and-found office.

Metric System

The metric system is used. Czechs use commas rather than decimal points, and points for thousands. Prices rounded to the nearest koruna are followed by a dash. See the conversion table following.

TEMPERATURE
°C = (°F - 32) ÷ 1.8
°F = (°C x 1.8) + 32

DISTANCE
1in = 2.54cm
1cm = 0.39in
1m = 3.3ft = 1.1yd
1ft = 0.3m
1km = 0.62 miles
1 mile = 1.6km

WEIGHT
1kg = 2.2lb
1lb = 0.45kg
1g = 0.04oz
1oz = 28g

VOLUME
1L = 0.26 US gallons
1 US gallon = 3.8L
1L = 0.22 imperial gallons
1 imperial gallon = 4.55L

Money
ATMS

There's no shortage of ATMs around Prague, particularly in busy shopping areas such as Na Příkopě, Wenceslas Square and náměstí Republiky, as well as the main train station and the airport. All ATMs will process cards belonging to, or affiliated with, Maestro, MasterCard, Visa, Plus and Cirrus.

CHANGING MONEY

The best place to change money is at one of the big banks, where commissions hover around 2%. The worst place is at one of the myriad private bureaux *(směnárna)* around Wenceslas Square and throughout the Old Town. Many of these advertise zero commission, which sounds terrific until you find out this percentage applies only to the selling of currency (ie selling you foreign currency in exchange for your koruna). When you are buying local currency, the commission charged can be as high as 10%. Try and avoid 5000Kč notes, as these can be difficult to change.

Banks are generally open 8am to 5pm Monday to Friday, but counters are sometimes temporarily unattended around lunchtime.

CURRENCY

The Czech currency is the koruna, contracted from *koruna česka* (crown) to Kč. Each koruna is divided into 100 *haléřů* (h; heller). Coins come in 50 haléřů, 1Kč, 2Kč, 5Kč, 10Kč and 20Kč pieces. Notes come in denominations of 50Kč, 100Kč, 200Kč, 500Kč, 1000Kč, 2000Kč and 5000Kč. The 50Kč coin exists but it is very scarce. Note that the near-worthless 10h and 20h coins have been withdrawn from circulation.

TRAVELLERS CHEQUES

Most mainstream tourist places accept travellers cheques from **American Express** (7, C2; ☎ 222 800 111) and **Thomas Cook** (4, D5; ☎ 221 105 371), but smaller businesses may refuse them.

Newspapers & Magazines

The main Czech-language daily newspapers include *Mladá fronta Dnes* and the conservative *Lidové noviny,* while the prime English-language newspaper is the slim, review-packed weekly *Prague Post*. There's also a German-language equivalent, the *Praguer Zeitung*. The gay-listings magazine *Amigo* is widely available at newsstands in the centre, as are many major international newspapers and magazines.

Photography & Video

Film-processing places are abundant, particularly in the Old Town and Malá Strana; try the professional Centrum Foto Škoda (p65). Entrust your slides to Fotographia Praha (4, E6) or to Fototechnika (4, F5); both use a reliable lab and are located in Lucerna Passage. Fototechnika is a dependable place for camera repairs.

The Czech Republic uses the PAL video system, which is incompatible with the Secam (France) or NTSC (Japan and North America) systems.

Post

Prague's postal service is fairly reliable, but for important items it's best to use registered mail *(do poručený dopis)* or Express Mail Service (EMS). The **main post office** (4, F5; ☎ 221 131 445; Jindřišská 14) has an automated queuing system. Entrance hall dispensers issue tickets; there are instructions in English on the machines, and an information desk inside the main hall to the left. Stamps can be bought at any newsstand.

POSTAL RATES

Standard mail to domestic destinations costs 7.50Kč. Postcards and letters to elsewhere in Europe cost 9Kč, and to Australia, USA and Canada 14Kč.

Radio

Local FM radio stations specialise in classical (Classic; 98.7), disco (Zlatá Praha; 97.2), pop (Bonton; 99.7) and hip alternative music (Radio 1; 91.9). The state-owned broadcaster is Czech Radio (Česky rozhlas; 92.6); its news bulletins are available daily at **Radio Prague** (www.radio.cz).

For English-language news and culture, simply switch over to the BBC World Service (101.1; www.bbc.cz), which rebroadcasts in Czech, Slovak and English. There's also Radio Free Europe (1233; 1287AM).

Telephone

All Czech telephone numbers have nine digits, and you must dial the full nine digits even if calling from the city. Using payphones for local calls at peak times (7am to 7pm Monday to Friday) costs around 4Kč for two minutes; rates fall by around 50% outside peak times. Note that blue phones only take coins (2Kč to 20Kč) but there are plenty of public phones that use phonecards (telekart) suitable for local, domestic and international calls.

Phonecards (200Kč and 300Kč) are available from the Prague Information Service (right), post offices and newsagents.

MOBILE PHONES

The mobile phone network is GSM 900, which is compatible with other European and Australian phones but not with Japanese or North American models (though GSM 1900 mobiles should work).

Television

There are two government-run TV channels, ČT1 and ČT2, the latter broadcasting the English-language 'Euronews' at either noon or 1pm. There are also two private channels, Nova and Prima, that show trashy sitcoms and soaps. Most hotels and rented apartments have satellite receivers.

Time

Czechs use the 24-hour clock. Prague Standard Time is one hour ahead of GMT/UTC. Daylight-savings time is from the last weekend in March to the last weekend of October.

Tipping

Some restaurants indicate on their menus or on your itemised bill that the final amount includes a tip; check to make sure you don't tip twice. If you feel the service warrants a gratuity, tip 10% to 15% extra.

Toilets

Public toilets (vé cé or toalet) for men (muži or páni) and women (ženy or dámy) in metro, train and bus station locations will normally be staffed by attendants, whose wages are paid by the 2Kč to 3Kč you give them for use of the facilities, although these places are seldom very clean. If you can, use the facilities at restaurants or in larger stores.

Tourist Information

The city-run **Prague Information Service** (Pražská informační služba, or PIS; 4, H5; ☎ 124 44; www.prague-info.cz) has four offices with information on the city; pick up the quarterly Welcome to Prague (45Kč) plus the free Prague This Month. Branches are at Old Town Hall (7, C2), Lucerna Passage (4, E6), the main train station (4, H5), and Malá Strana Bridge Tower (4, A3; Mostecká 2; ☾ closed Nov-Mar).

The private **Prague Tourist Centre** (7, D4; ☎ 224 212 209; www.ptc.cz; Rytířská 12) sells guidebooks, maps and tickets to concerts and theatre around town.

Women Travellers

Compared with other large European cities, Prague is a safe city for women, but there has been a rise in the incidence of sexual violence towards women in the past decade, and verbal harassment is not uncommon.

Women, particularly solo travellers, may find many neighbourhood pubs less enjoyable because of their complete domination by macho types. Don't worry there are still plenty of relaxed vinárny (wine bars) and alcohol-serving kavárny (cafés) to discover.

LANGUAGE

Czech (čeština) is obviously the main language spoken in the Czech Republic. English is widespread in central Prague but not commonly spoken in the outer suburbs and the countryside – 'widespread' doesn't mean 'always', however, and you'll often encounter people in the tourist industry who speak very little or no English. Many older citizens also speak German.

Originating from a west Slavonic linguistic grouping, Czech can be a mouthful for first-time speakers, particularly trying to pronounce the words that are vowel-free zones. However, it doesn't take that long to begin getting the hang of some of the more commonly used words and phrases, and the effort is often appreciated by locals. For a more detailed look at the language, get a copy of Lonely Planet's *Czech Phrasebook*.

Useful Words & Phrases

Good day.	*Dobrý den.*
Goodbye.	*Na shledanou.*
Hello/Goodbye.	*Ahoj/Čau.*
How are you?	*Jak se máte?*
Fine, thanks.	*Děkuji, dobře.*
Yes.	*Ano/Jo.*
No.	*Ne.*
Excuse me.	*S dovolením.*
Sorry.	*Promiňte.*
Please.	*Prosím.*
Thank you very much.	*Mockrát děkuji.*
That's fine/ You're welcome.	*Neni zač.*
Do you speak English?	*Mluvíte anglicky?*
I don't understand.	*Nerozumím.*

Getting Around

What time does... leave/arrive?	*V kolik hodin odjíždí/přijíždí...?*
the train	*vlak*
the bus	*autobus*
Which platform?	*Které nástupiště?*
Excuse me, where is...?	*Prosím, kde je...?*
I'm looking for... (the) ticket office	*Hledám... pokladna*
I want to go to...	*Chci jet do...*
Go straight ahead.	*Jděte přímo.*
Turn left.	*Zatočte vlevo.*
Turn right.	*Zatočte vpravo.*

Buying Tickets

I'd like...	*Rád (m) bych...* *Ráda (f) bych...*
a one-way ticket	*jednosměrnou jízdenku*
a return ticket	*zpáteční jízdenku*
two tickets	*dvě jízdenky*

Accommodation

Do you have any rooms available?	*Máte volné pokoje?*
I'd like...	*Přál (m) bych si...* *Přála (f) bych si...*
a single room	*jednolůžkový pokoj*
a double room	*dvoulůžkový pokoj*
How much is it per night?	*Kolik stojí jedna noc?*

Around Town

bank	*banka*
embassy	*velvyslanectví*
information centre	*informační centrum*
main square	*hlavní náměstí*
market	*tržiště/trh*
theatre	*divadlo*
train station	*ČD/železniční nádraží*

Time & Dates

What time is it?	*Kolik je hodin?*
When?	*Kdy?*
in the morning	*ráno*
in the afternoon	*odpoledne*
in the evening	*večer*
today	*dnes*
now	*ted'*
Monday	*pondělí*
Tuesday	*úterý*
Wednesday	*středa*
Thursday	*čtvrtek*
Friday	*pátek*
Saturday	*sobota*
Sunday	*neděle*
January	*leden*
February	*únor*
March	*březen*

April	*duben*
May	*květen*
June	*červen*
July	*červenec*
August	*srpen*
September	*září*
October	*říjen*
November	*listopad*
December	*prosinec*

Numbers

0	*nula*
1	*jeden*
2	*dva*
3	*tři*
4	*čtyři*
7	*sedm*
8	*osm*
9	*devět*
10	*deset*
50	*padesát*
5	*pět*
6	*šest*
100	*sto*
1000	*tisíc*

Emergencies

Help!	*Pomoc!*
I'm ill.	*Jsem nemocný/ nemocná.* (m/f)
Please call a doctor.	*Prosím, zavolejte doktora.*
ambulance	*sanitku*
police	*policii*
Where is the toilet?	*Kde je záchod?*
I'm lost.	*Zabloudil/ a jsem.* (m/f)
Could you help me please?	*Prosím, můžete mi pomoci?*

Index

FEATURES

🍴	C'est La Vie	*Eating*
🎭	Black Light Theatre	*Entertainment*
🍺	Bloody Freddy Bar	*Drinking*
☕	Café Screen	*Café*
🏛	Strahov Monastery	*Highlights*
🛍	Art Décoratif	*Shopping*
🏰	Troja Chateau	*Sights/Activities*
🏨	Hotel Paříž	*Sleeping*

AREAS

	Building
	Land
	Mall
	Market
	Other Area
	Park/Cemetery
	Urban

HYDROGRAPHY

	River, Creek
	Intermittent River
	Canal
	Water

BOUNDARIES

	State, Provincial
	Regional, Suburb
	Ancient Wall

ROUTES

	Tollway
	Freeway
	Primary Road
	Secondary Road
	Tertiary Road
	Lane
	One-Way Street
	Unsealed Road
	Mall/Steps
	Tunnel
	Walking Path
	Walking Trail/Track
	Pedestrian Overpass
	Walking Tour

TRANSPORT

✈	Airport, Airfield
🚌	Bus Route
	Funicular
⛴	Ferry
	General Transport
Ⓜ	Metro
	Monorail
	Rail
	Taxi Rank
	Tram

SYMBOLS

🏦		Bank, ATM
🏰		Castle, Fortress
✝		Christian
		Embassy, Consulate
✚		Hospital, Clinic
ℹ		Information
@		Internet Access
✡		Jewish
🗼		Lighthouse
		Lookout
		Monument
▲		Mountain
		National Park
Ⓟ		Parking Area
		Petrol Station
●		Point of Interest
		Police Station
		Post Office
		Ruin
☎		Telephone
🚻		Toilets
♿		Wheelchair Access
🐦		Zoo, Bird Sanctuary

24/7 travel advice
www.lonelyplanet.com